Dedication

To Mary Jo, my ever-supportive wife.

To the one who influenced my studious habits,
Professor Dr. E. M. Blaiklock.

To my mother Ella Winger-Lincoln, who introduced me to the
love of books.

I0161568

Contents

Introduction — The Journey We Are About to Take

Here's an age old remedy for the diseases of the mind. Change the way you think, and you change who you are. Change who you are, and you change the world around you. It won't work, you say? Well, maybe you don't know what to change, or how to change it, or even why what we think and say becomes so readily us.

You may have wondered at times why your children don't act and think like you. That's because they are different. But also, they are being subjected unwittingly to a brainwashing of sorts. Our culture is the agent. Your children are so easily influenced by technology, its games, its language, the films they see, and the world you don't want them to see or hear. As children, they do not have the wherewithal to make a sensible judgment. It's a constant fight to correct the wrong and unhelpful influences that this technologically driven culture has brought into the home. Can the parent do anything in the wake of this tsunami that has swept across our minds? Yes! So, what do you do and where do you start? We will find out.

We call this invasion of our lives "our changing culture." It's not just children but also adults who have unthinkingly absorbed these influences. Adults are at a loss to detect the slipperiness of crooked thinking and to possess the knowhow to form convincing arguments that expose its intentional deception. It doesn't take long before children and adults are thinking differently. When we don't see the dishonesty, it becomes a dangerous virus of the mind. We don't need the latest research to tell us what we have been told for millenniums: "As a man thinketh in his heart, so is he." Of course, that means men and women. And if you thought the word *thinketh* is either outdated English or a translation from another language, you would be right. It's from a Hebrew proverb. Research on who and how humans function tells us the proverb is right on target.

What we think and how we think soon becomes our language. Our language, too, changes with our thinking. We are even being told today what is politically correct speech and what is not. That's a red flag, warning us of the loss of mental freedom. Conversation has degraded today to a low level not taught and modeled so convincingly since the early days of the Greeks. Politicians, ideologists, and philosophers lead on this slippery slope of crooked thinking.

Fraudulent thinking has never elevated a culture. The lying, deceit, and shameless selling to the unwary public (particularly the youth) of counterfeit arguments is commonplace now. It is an intellectual sleight of hand and is perpetuated in our institutions of higher learning. Our children do not posses the knowledge to detect its dishonest trickery. Adults also, at times, do not know what is dishonest and what is sound logic and trustworthy thinking. Help is found in the pages ahead.

This book is designed to, first, inform how we got to where we are. It will support parents with help to guide and train their children's minds as they continue to watchfully guide and care for their physical health and development. Little correction of the crooked thinking is found in the educational systems. Seldom is honest thinking even taught.

Tired of being lied to? Tired of getting angry with your children's devious arguments? Tired of all the questionable "help" your child is getting from others? The simple tools and takeaway points that follow each chapter are the starting place for your becoming the PI of false thinking and the model of straight thinking. One might say, becoming the guide to the personal honesty and freedom of your child's mind and your own can become your mission.

This book is not a philosophical treatise, although it will now and then point to the cause of spurious thinking that is born in the minds of biased philosophers. It is written so that the lay person will grasp and will be able to use the knowledge to change their own thinking, if needed, and help correct the thinking of others.

- "Adults and *parents on a mission*" is a good mission statement for this book and the reason for reading it.
- Parents who want an education into the task of parenting are offered here the tools to help.

＊＊＊＊＊

We begin our journey with a reminder that reason as well as emotion forms the foundation of a solid faith or belief — the use of head and heart. But if reason is to be a part of faith's solid and logical foundation, we need to understand how to think clearly and accurately.

We think all day long. Most never know how to think in an effective manner, as opposed to a ineffective manner. We should develop a passion to learn more about how to think straight and how to be able to spot those false and deceptive arguments that convince many of us, especially our youth. To give our children the skill of straight thinking and to teach them to spot false thinking are priceless trainings parents can offer.

We are what we think and this hint to an effective methodology is the way crooked thinkers are changing the culture of our day. The methodology is not wrong, but the use of it is blatantly, at times, deceptive. It easily convinces our youth of ideas that are false to the core. Our use of the same method places parents in the seat of being prime influencers for our children's full and effective use of their mental faculties. Keep the family unit strong and influential!

A glance at the Contents will suggest the mental landscape through which we will travel. It is my hope that you will approach this book with an open mind, not biased by the incentives of specious educators. The deception that has influenced much of our thinking has been "wise as a serpent" is wise.

Use the common sense tools to reframe your thinking. Remember, common sense is not a way of thinking that is uneducated. It is uneducated to ignore its evidence in favor of ideas that have little or no foundation in truth and fact.

1 – Half a Faith Won't Do!

Parents are frustrated and hurting with the challenges of the current dysfunctional culture. It is dysfunctional because it contradicts itself and encourages our youth to believe in an angry, self-centered, and crooked (read "unthinking") way of living. It claims all people must be tolerant of others, but then it is not tolerant of beliefs it disagrees with! There is a word for that: hypocrisy.

This hypocrisy would eliminate all meganarratives (a meganarrative is one that claims to apply to all people). Today's proponents of postmodernist philosophy are targeting, in particular Christianity, which they claim to be a meganarrative and is what they say is wrong with the world of our day. Parents must see their significant role in helping to stem the flow of this "re-education" of our youth that results in a culture forced on all of us. Change the thinking of our youth and these postmodern thinkers know they will effectively change our world. It is, to give it an honest label, irrational thinking and a destructive amoral culture, where even freedom is falsely pedaled as absolute.

Our culture is taking us down a path constructed by off-beat thinkers. They falsify who we are and rob our youth — all of us — of a healthy and uplifting self-image. It is a culture that will destroy any peaceful society and establish a way of thinking that marginalizes truth, common sense, reason, and all mega-narratives.

Is your faith a faith of the heart and not the head? We need a faith of the head as well as the heart to be able to explain and defend the beliefs that run counter to this culture. Our beliefs must be founded in what is reasonable (the head) and in intelligent emotions (the heart). Too many people are lacking the strength of a head belief (a reason for their beliefs) and when the culture begins to demean the human being or make no sense, they have no valid rational defense to support what they believe. Hence, they are losing the argument of why it is intelligent to believe what they believe by default. Our children must be equipped to think straight. Don't depend on the educational system to teach them this. Not even all universities take the trouble to teach students how to think — unbelievable, but true.

We need sound thinking and successful reasons to defend what we believe.

The classic story of facts and feelings (head and heart) could well be the story of the disciple Thomas. Jesus appeared to the disciples after his resurrection and Thomas, on this occasion, was present. Instead of rebuking Thomas for his lack of belief, Jesus offered him the evidence he needed to be convinced. "Reach out your hand and place your finger in the nail prints… and be not faithless but believing," he said. The convincing of the mind by the presentation of rational evidence is essential to the development of a complete belief — head and heart, facts and feelings.

- We are what we think and feel. Both head (thinking) and heart (feeling) make up the thinking activity of our minds. Some of us lean more toward thoughts and others more toward feelings.

- In the story of Thomas, we could say he leaned more toward thinking and used his head more than his heart. In his mind, he thought it was irrational to think that anyone could rise from the dead, so he had to have evidence that it had happened or it would not be a part of his beliefs. We tend to mostly make our decisions one way or the other. Thoughts deal mainly with known facts, and feelings are solely responses of our limbic system (our brain's emotional circuitry).

- Head is not more valuable than heart and we must learn to value and operate each, managing them and bringing them under our control so that neither controls us[1].

- Heart is not made up of just our feelings but is also made up of our beliefs. Beliefs are formed from our values, and what we value and believe are what we call our faith or our beliefs. But faith must be built on reason — on rational, logical thinking. And that is why we will take a moment and learn how to think straight rather than in a crooked, uneducated, irrational way.

The validity of *a* head faith is based on verifiable evidence and sound thinking. *Straight and Crooked Thinking* is the title of Robert H. Thouless' classic, first published in 1930[2] — a book I read when in my teens. I recommend it. So, let's use his title and define straight and crooked thinking.

What Is Straight Thinking?
If we are going to have a faith built on evidence, we will need straight (rational, logical) thinking to comprise a convincing and loving presentation. If we are going to convince our

---

[1] See *Intelligently Emotional* by Ray W. Lincoln for a fuller understanding of how to control and manage our emotions.

[2] The book is now available in an updated edition by his grandson C. R. Thouless.

youth, we must also have watertight arguments and not forget to model the facts of which we are seeking to convince them.

Straight thinking is thinking…

- Factually (which means with all the facts fairly represented).

- Accurately (which means telling the whole truth and nothing but the truth about all the facts, not just some of the facts, as is often done when the arguments are specious). Arguments that have the ring of truth but are, in reality, misleading are the stock-in-trade of modern day sophists.

- Truthfully (which means without falsification and twisting of the facts).

- Honestly (which includes being motivated by honesty as well as being honest). An honest basis for reasoning starts in the heart, in our love for others.

- Representing reality (not building a case on speculation, fantasy, or imagination while passing it off as truth).

- Verifiably (meaning using facts that can be evidentially verified). Evidence is found in our physical universe (including all the minutest details of living creatures) and in our valid experiences, not forgetting our subjective realities.

- Consistently (meaning without contradiction or flipping your position, like politicians often do). It requires presenting your reasons without changing them in midstream to avoid being trapped. This consistency is the bread and butter of a solid argument.

- Unadulterated by irrelevant facts (means don't divert from the point being discussed by changing the discussion to facts that are not relevant. Don't chase irrelevant rabbits so that the discussion is diverted to trivial details).

- Justly (meaning what is fair and impartial).

- Logically (what we will call straight thinking and the opposite of crooked thinking). Logical thinking is thinking from accurate and defensible assumptions, then constructing logically rational arguments on your assumption. This, you will find plenty of examples of in this book. If you need to, you will learn straight thinking as you read.

Unfortunately, the way of thinking that lies behind the latest changes to our culture fails on all these counts. Postmodernism and its accepted theories, materialism and natural selection, are a classic example of trampling all over straight and logical thinking[3].

What Is Crooked Thinking?

Our thinking is inaccurate, dishonest, or crooked when we say or do any or all of the following.

Crooked thinking is…
- Saying, "Everyone thinks this," when everyone doesn't, or "Everyone does it," when everyone doesn't (an argument parents are familiar with), or "We all know this to be a fact," when it is not universally believed. This is called stretching the truth, exaggeration, and sometimes, blatant lying in the

---

[3] A brief discussion and exposure of Postmodernist thinking is an upcoming feature in the author's blog.

hope no one will fact check us. When citing common sense, it is a valid argument only if those listening to you agree that it is commonly held to be sensible.

- Fastening on a trivial point in the discussion while avoiding the main issue. Declaring the whole argument to be false because a minor divergence from accuracy is observed.

- Arguing that a dubious point is universally accepted when, in fact, it isn't universally accepted.

- Resorting to illogical reasoning based on false assumptions. This invalidates the whole argument. The assumption must be restated accurately, and the reasoning must possess the ability to support the restated assumption.

- Manipulating people's emotions by making shocking statements that cannot be defended or do not represent the whole truth in order to get people to believe what is being argued. Because emotions are usually a part of an argument, they must not be given more importance than the emotions should rightly have.

- Using one's education or status to claim validity for ones own statements. This is hiding behind status or education and asking to be believed.

The thinking that lies behind the latest changes to our culture uses these "crooked" tactics to convince us of their beliefs and fails to be concerned about straight thinking. Straight thinking is not needed in the minds of postmodernists, because they do not value or accept the validity of reason and logic, reality and truth. We can still use straight thinking to dispute their arguments. But understand, we should first have determined the real reasons why our listener is holding firm to their position. Sometimes, emotional reasons are dominant, and these need to be shown to be of less value than the truth and what it offers us, or we will not succeed in challenges to their opinions.

Most of these irrational tactics are easily detectable, so be your own judge. However, often, dishonest people will also twist the truth and only partly represent it to achieve their goals. This is called *sophistry*, a way to deceive people that was taught to the Greeks as early in our history as 600 BC. This is why we take the oath in court to speak the whole truth and nothing but the truth — no bending or inadequate representation of the truth allowed. Deception is to be ferreted out and truth, alone, used to form a just verdict. Courts are supposed to be charged with finding the truth.

All of us need to be straight thinkers and truth finders. Sometimes, because of the flawed and contradictory nature of the conversation, we need to take a little time to understand fully what has been said. However, to be rational, we have to be straight thinkers.

Our goal? Not to be fooled by contrived arguments that mean to deceive, having the ring of truth and plausibility but which, in reality, are fallacious. Spurious arguments, which are obviously false but phrased is such a way to hide their deception, make up some of the things people believe because they have accepted them uncritically. Misleading and false understandings of who we are and how we should live are driving the changes in our culture. They can be discredited by sound, straight thinking. So, speak the truth, but…(read on)

Speak the Truth in Love

Straight thinking is to be presented in a loving and patient way or it will be rejected by the listener from the start. This could be labeled a ubiquitous reason because all of us, parents included, must speak the truth in obvious love and concern for our children and all people. Why? Because all humans have been made awesomely in "the image of God." We must learn that only obvious love for those we may disagree with will help open their closed minds and hearts to who they really are and what they can be.

Make the Family a Unit Where Minds Are Made Strong

It's not just the culture, but Western civilization that is breaking down. How do we know that? Family, the basic unit of society, is suffering. You can't destroy or degrade the importance of the unit on which society and the human race is built without distorting what humans think about themselves — all humans. Parents struggle to raise their children in the face of powerful and appealing influences from outside the home that use subtle, crooked thinking to win people over. These influences are often more impacting on a child's upbringing than the values parents strive to instill. Influences from outside are not new, but they are more impacting in the fast moving society of the last few decades.

Let's say it again: family is the basic unit in all societies and it is where the human race continually finds its new beginnings. It is where children are born and raised and where, in their most formative years, they develop values and beliefs that mold their lives for decades to come, if not for their entire lives. The future shape of a nation is predictable by the values, morals, and beliefs it teaches its children and the way in which it nurtures the moral health of its families.

But no longer can a family feel that it is the main influence in a child's mental and moral upbringing. And don't shy at the word *moral*. All amoral cultures have imploded and destroyed themselves. History is our teacher, if we will listen to its practical wisdom.

Parents Face Choices

A changing culture, with its contradictory and questionable beliefs, is competing with a parent's desire to teach sound values and what they see as the wisdom their children need. Competition means choices. As never before, the free access to unguided information, disseminated everywhere in our technological age (even, at times, in our schools), has provided easy and tempting access for immature minds. The young child's ever-hungry curiosity and sense of wonder stores, without educated caution, things it has no rational or moral compass to evaluate.

To further challenge the parent, an educational system that is influenced by postmodernist thinking, plus an entertainment world that is influenced by the same philosophy, and their revolutionary impact on our children and youth, have changed the way people in general think — and certainly not always for the good. We are all aware of how many ideas have failed in education alone in just the past 50 years. Things are changing, but not always for the good of our world. Be aware!

Societies, governed by politics that have been strategically infiltrated by postmodernist thinking, can be quick to trash the values of the past in favor of the latest untested ideas. A

13

changing culture progresses the same as all knowledge does: "one funeral of ideas after another." All progress advances in this manner. However, we all discover, at times, that the baby has been thrown out with the bath water. When children are raised with false narratives of how to live peacefully in a healthy society, the future of both the society and the individual is at risk. This book will introduce you to some of the latest beliefs that are influencing our youth and how you can combat them successfully as parents who want to raise their children to think straight for themselves.

Freedom — A Commonly Misrepresented Idea

We are living in a society that teaches our children false narratives about, for example, the meaning of freedom. How do we know this? By observing the behavior of children who feel they have absolute freedom to treat others (parents included) in any way they feel they want to.

True freedom is to act in such a way as to benefit ourselves and others. Never is it license to act disparagingly of parents or others. When talking with parents, I constantly find their most pressing concern is the disrespect they receive from their children. Frustrating to the parent is their child's repudiation of their attempts to correct such behavior. These actions are becoming more frequent and alarming than ever before. Parents are understandably frustrated and angered, not knowing what to do. Many have tried all they know, and still the freedom to talk and act dis-respectfully in most homes persists and gets worse as the child enters teenage. It is blatantly obvious that the influences of our society are permeating our homes. In a healthy society, freedom is not a right to act in any way we feel like in the moment.

Such crooked thinking about freedom will not prepare our children to create in their generation a safe, healthy, and beneficial adult society. Anger, disrespect of others, payback, and violence is the fruit that hangs on the tree of a misconceived notion of freedom.

Freedom is also being worshipped today as something that is an absolute right, no matter the ill results of its wrong use. We are told the freedom to express ourselves as we please is the only way to be real and true to ourselves, and people of any age should not be denied it. That crooked thinking is a recipe for unbridled disrespect of others. The result has obviously changed behavior in schools and homes. Its full bloom is being seen in violent acts and demonstrations, where people want to change things according to their own desires and beliefs, regardless of how it damages others. Our world has seen more than it wants of this attitude running wild.

The culture we are living in also venerates the freedom to deny facts in favor of feelings. A fool can see that we can't raise children to respect the rights of others when influences invade the home (actually, they come from within some homes), teaching the children they have a right to respond as they will to their emotional urges — in many cases, to do whatever they please. In a healthy society we are not free to abuse the bodies or rights and emotional health of others, and that includes the actions of parents, of course[4]. Our actions, when they are the result of crooked thinking, teach a child in the way they should *not* go and they will not depart from it. We are not free to do whatever we want without consequences or to treat our parents in a way we would hate

---

[4] I am not speaking here of needed disciplinary actions. That is another subject.

to be treated. The influences felt by a child in its formative years are long lasting. It's not just this abuse of parents; it is all the other issues that degrade who we are as humans and as a race.

A correct assessment must be made of what is causing this re-evaluation of personal rights, this tolerance of ideologies that want to destroy values and replace them with unproven ideas that, even before they start injecting them into our culture, make no sense. The proponents of these ideas do not practice what they preach. Think about that. Because these thinkers cannot and do not live the beliefs they preach, it should flag all of us that something is false about their teachings. And we have addressed only one example of our culture's foul smelling results that is forced on our culture with crooked thinking.

Where is this current thinking coming from? Not from where most people imagine, but from philosophers. Philosophy produces ideologies and new ways of thinking. It is the driving power behind the cultural change by creating new beliefs that have only a semblance of reality. These ways of thinking must be confronted and their falseness challenged or our youth and all of us will unwittingly swallow a bitter toxin. Postmodernism, which embraces materialism and natural selection, are largely responsible for the culture in which we are living. Of course, we should not be against change, but we should draw the line at destructive changes.

Most importantly, this book will give parents the practical tools to remedy these false beliefs and specious ways of thinking. Here is the path, parents, to reducing your "pain" and to helping your children to become straight thinkers.

2 — A Glimpse of What Is and Is to Come

Tired of being sassed by your children? Have you noticed that behind this behavior is the reality that they don't think any longer like you do? Have you even suffered obnoxious disrespect? I know this takes place, to some degree, in almost every home. But what can you do about it and the apparent escalation? Anything? When talking with parents, that's the hot question I get asked all the time? Some explain it more mildly this way: How do I combat the widening gap between me and the changing culture that my kids are living in?

Another request from parents is for a path to immediate gratification. We want quick fixes, but there is no quick fix to the tsunami of influences coming via technology, iPhones, chrome books, computers, video games, the media, internet, social media, and films. The values they espouse are, to say the very least, subversive of traditional values.

Is there something behind this widespread attempt to change our culture? Most definitely!
Parents are worried that their children are being educated more by their peers and the constant exposure to a destructive culture that has much more free access into their kids minds than they do. Have you waved the white flag, yet, and just given up, not knowing what to do?

Perhaps, we are not asking the right questions. Let's try this one: What has caused these dramatic changes in our culture? Changes have filtered down to the minds of our children and our teens and ushered in a new, and I will argue, a divisive culture. These changes are taking away the influence of parents, who are being reduced to caretakers of their children, who are then influenced and educated by (in some schools) the state's ideas of what is right for our world. A closer look at what is happening reveals beliefs that are even demeaning to the dignity of humans and, if we understand its intent, a path to the downgrading of our humanness. We could put the question this way, "What is the underlying cause of what we are experiencing as a cultural upheaval — or should we call it a revolution?" Remember the wise advice, "Don't deal with the symptoms; find the cause and deal with that." First, however, we must know what the cause is.

The Cause

The cause is, as I have indicated already, a different way of thinking, fed to our youth by "appealing" beliefs that are subtly presented. It has achieved what we have already seen: a state of affairs, accepted and blindly tolerated in the culture of our Western countries. The methods and goals are the same as those the practice of brainwashing uses: to take the mind captive. Undoubtedly, this is a successful path to changing behavior because we are what we think.

Postmodernism and its foundational beliefs have already won the battle for the minds of those in places of significant influence — namely, in the educational and political spheres. It is winning the minds of our children as a result. It undermines patriotism and family by placing the power of freedom in the hands of the individual. That individual is your child in many cases. Parents are, to say the least, frustrated at their loss of acknowledged and effective authority. The writers of our culture are the individuals driving the energy behind social justice for what they see as oppressed groups

— groups distinguished by race, gender, ethnicity, sexual identity, and any self-declared social unit whose agendas are mistakenly thought to be for the universal good of mankind. What these writers are doing is clearly for *their* own good. Change the way people think and you can change the world. Begin with the young and you change generation after generation. Counter these damaging changes in the minds of the young and you counter this destructive progress. Parents must enter the struggle and regain their rightful and loving authority.

The postmodernist changes to our culture began to take effect around 1970 and have slowly taken over much of the thinking in higher education, schools, politics, and almost all aspects of our lives. Here are some of the results of this thinking as it affects our world and our children. You may discover its subtle changes in the way you, also, think at times. I have chosen a few of Postmodernism's beliefs and their results that are obvious in our culture as a sneak preview of this new reality. "Help" and "how to's" for parents are to be found in the chapters ahead, but for now, a first impression.

There Is No Truth That Applies to Everyone — A License to Behave the Way You Wish

Western society was built on the fact that there are truths that apply to everyone. We call them universal or absolute truths. Can you think of some? The police operate on some, and all parents are certain there have to be some, too. The changes in our culture teach the opposite: there is no absolute or universal truth that can be true for all people. Have you heard something like this: "What's true for you does not have to be true for me," or "If I see it differently from you, don't tell me I am wrong," or "My opinion or the way I see it is my truth," or "Right and wrong is whatever I think it is"? Sounds liberating, and in this freedom lies its appeal. But all that liberates does not necessarily build a safe, responsible, effective, or considerate way of living.

We are asked to believe the sweeping claim "All statements that are said to apply to all people are simply not true." That's what we call an assumption, a basic precept that is the foundation for an argument. If the assumption is not true, game over. What's the problem with this way of thinking? The assumption on which the argument depends is simply not true. That's what is wrong. Build an argument on a false fact or truth, and your argument is false. See how essential being truthful and thinking straight are?

Let's test this way of thinking that says, "No truth applies to everyone and all statements that apply to everyone are simply not true." It's very crooked thinking. Here is the evidence of its spuriousness. There are countless things that are true for all of us. The law of gravity is true for everyone. Test it. "Everyone has to eat and drink" is true for all. This reality exists and is a truth about our world, applying to everyone, that we had better not forget. Again, try living as though reality does not exist, if you don't believe in it. No one can and no one does!

Here are more. Consequences are real. All decisions entail consequences. Give this one a wack! A rock is real and its hardness is real. Try giving it a good punch with your fist if you don't believe it applies to everyone. You will quickly become a believer in the reality of reality. Love is superior to hatred, and if you don't believe that, try treating all your friends with hatred and see how many friends you have left. When your assumption is not true, your thinking is crooked and patently false.

Now consider how crooked the thinking of the Postmodernism is. Postmodernism is the philosophy of our day and it wants us to believe the opposite of what the real world and common sense demand of us. The consequences of these beliefs can damage our lives severely and rob us of happiness. In the case of the examples above, our thinking must undergo a turn around, and our lives also if all this is true.

The postmodernist also uses this crooked way of thinking to announce that Christianity is not true. How? Because they claim its truths apply to us all — which they do. But how is that evidence that Christianity is not true? Their thinking is even more crooked than the Three Sister roads in the Texas Hill Country.

They call Christianity a mega-narrative because it makes universal claims, as I have said, and they tell us they despise all meganarratives. (However, note their resort to crooked thinking: they condemn *all meganarratives* and then make exceptions, first, for all their own universal claims and second, for the universal claims of a few religions they favor, such as Islam[5]. The postmodern culture exempts Islam as the footnote makes clear).

That's called a self-refuting argument, because it refutes itself. It says one can't make this claim and then promptly makes the same claim for themselves. In cases like this, their own claim just shot them in the foot. Teach your children the

------

[5] One example of Islam being allowed to be taught in public schools was reported in World Net Daily December 23, 2003, — "Judge rules Islamic Education OK in California Schools," while the Christian prayer and teaching was outlawed. Read more shocking hypocritical occurrences in other states as cited in *Dark Agenda*, by David Horowitz, Chapter 5.

hypocrisy of what is happening. Parents may need to learn how crooked their own thinking is at times so they can then model straight thinking for their children and educate them about the duplicity of these new cultural demands. If we, as parents, model it, they will begin to take us more seriously.

Science makes universal claims, too. Therefore, the claims of science are also not true according to Postmodernist thinking. It should be easy to debunk such spurious thinking and behavior. Of course, if the person you are trying to influence has battened down the hatches of their mind, or has retreated to claim the protection of their status and their ivory tower, they will not listen. They are the educated elite and whatever they say is what you must believe. Teach your children how to think straight from their earliest years. Straight is the only really educated way to think.

Social Justice — Change the Legal System! But to What?

You have no doubt heard the words "social justice," but you may not fully understand their significance. It is a legal attempt to let the offender off, or lighten their punishment because they had a challenging childhood, or to bend the law to accommodate some social group's "truth" about how they feel they have been treated. **We are being told that even the legal system's laws should not apply equally to us all —** another untested and unworkable assumption for which there is no corroborating evidence. The history of human behavior is solidly against such an idea, but these tried and true facts are being ignored.

Children love this unequal way of handling things whenever they have been caught breaking the home's rules. Their thinking has been influenced by the statement "the rules do not apply equally to all people." Therefore, they see responsibility and accountability as the parent's tools to beat them up. They have also seen the way laws across the land are being applied differently by different judges. If judges don't agree and parents don't agree and even schools apply the rules differently, using social justice as their excuse, why should parents be so rigid and unbending? To add to the child's pile of ammunition is the fact that all the parents of their peers don't apply the rules in the same way all the time, either. The majority of parents are frustrated with their efforts to hold their children accountable and when facing the child's anger, they wave the white flag. They then tend to claim their love and care was the motivation for their surrendering to the child's tirade.

There is a genuine problem here. Where does being responsible and accountable begin and end? Likewise, where does love and grace and a parent's commitment to caring begin and end? Are there some exceptions and what are they? These are the reasons why these issues need to be clearly understood. Children are smart. They quickly explore all possibilities. "My sister asked me to do it for her." "I'm the youngest and I did not know it was wrong." "If Mom hadn't made me so angry, I wouldn't have done it." They claim the rule does not apply to them because someone or something is to blame, not them. Sound familiar?

The legal system solved this problem by first determining guilt or innocence beyond a reasonable doubt. So, the charged person was either right or wrong, guilty or not guilty beyond a reasonable doubt. Then the judge had certain flexibility in determining the severity of the sentence. How is this different from social justice? Social justice determines the fate of the one charged before the legal process begins, based not on the law but on the person's claims for either dismissal or leniency determined by their social status or privilege. The deterrent is, then, not a matter for the legal system but for some ideology to determine. Ideology, in these cases, has trumped equality in the court room.

Another problem exists today. The postmodern way of thinking gives more support for someone who is actually guilty to blame others for their wrong doing. "My truth is what applies to me and the way I see it" or simply, "I'm not to blame." "There is no truth that applies to everyone equally and the way it applies to me is different. I am the exception and I will explain why, but I shouldn't have to explain." We have entered a new postmodern era in our culture where justice is now being redefined and the term "social justice" (meaning the appeal to the social and individual conditions and opinions of the offender) rewrites the law in the offender's favor. Happy thought — for them! One thing consistently seems to be lost in the definition of social justice. That is insistence on personal responsibility for our actions and, in the face of personal responsibility, a just and fair result for both the offender and the offended. Something is crooked when the offender is favored over the offended.

Laws that apply to all of us, not to a favored few, are the best humans can do when it comes to justice. Social justice is crooked thinking. Only God, who knows all the facts and conditions that were relevant to the offense and the offended, can therefore make the kind of judgment that calls for a perfect balance between justice and mercy.

Under social justice's flexible interpretation of the law, your child can claim you are not just or fair if you do not consider their complaints about how you have failed in your parenting — conditions they could construe and they can claim as part of being treated by the principles of social justice. Why then does social justice deliver an imperfect judgment? Because humans do not know all the facts and conditions like God does, and the claim to our right to be treated differently is an escape from justice, not a plea for its enactment. Social justice, as we see it enacted, often ends up failing to arrive at true justice for all concerned.

Any perceived faults on your part as parents become grounds for the child receiving a lighter consequence, or none at all. "You are mean or simply wrong, with all those rules, laws, and consequences applying equally to all members of the family." This is the way your child is thinking and they are doing so with conviction that they are right under the application of social justice. To be fair to all is only possible when the law applies equally to all. A culture that excuses personal responsibility encourages crime. Many in socially poor neighborhoods have shown how personal responsibility triumphs. They have carved out for themselves notable and praiseworthy lives without the need for claiming exemptions based on their conditions.

Our children's minds are sponges, soaking up the differences in the way the school treats its students and the way their parents and peer's parents treat their kids. Not forgetting, they are bombarded by the daily news of how people use anger and violence against all who don't agree with them. Sometimes, this is the model they see in the home as their parents play the blame game between themselves. This behavior is represented as something that is somehow justifiable. Hence, they feel justified in being angry at you.

Morals Are Personally Decided. Deviant Behavior Is Self Expression. Really?

Once we work from the assumption that there are no universal or absolute truths, we are left with no ground for morals or standards for socially acceptable behavior. Good and bad become morally equal. Normal and deviant merge. Deviant behavior is mostly defended as being a healthy form of self expression and self expression is surely a healthy behavior. Society is now being reconstructed around this premise. Standards are needed because unrestrained deviant behavior opens wide the path to unrestrained development of passion and desire. Without restraints or standards, emotions rule and rational sense is placed on the back burner.

No society has ever been able to sustain itself without universal truths, especially moral truths. Freedom to behave the way we want leads to division, fighting, and revengeful actions. We can't deny or try to hide the facts of how humans behave when unrestrained. Although there are historians who won't admit it, the fall of the Roman Empire was in large part due to the utter collapse of moral standards. Moral anarchy reigned in what used to be a disciplined and restrained culture. The Roman culture collapsed.

Promises are gutted at the whim of the next moment's emotions. "My word is my bond" becomes "My word is my warning to not trust me. You should know better than to trust. I am not binding myself to some promise. I am free to break promises if I want to." Under those conditions, everything would have to be a contract. But even a contract is undermined without accountability to moral standards. Admittedly, all humans fail to keep all of their promises. But a society in which a promise is fundamentally not a promise must also look favorably on having no integrity at its core. So ask yourself, is a world in which no integrity or standards of behavior are commonly required a world in which you would want to live?

Some postmodernists are promoting the idea of having a contract between child and parent as the basis for child-parent relationships! If no standards apply to all people, that also includes kids, we are told. When the moral standards and common sense of the good in the bygone parenting culture are abandoned, we are left with contracts that will also fail for the same reasons. The era when young children were recognized as still not physically and mentally able to make wise moral choices by themselves recognized that the authority and training of parents was needed and worked. Who doesn't agree that parents should be able to establish better boundaries than kids? The number of people that are agreeing that the State can do a better job than the kids' parents in establishing boundaries and freedoms for kids is growing under truly crooked and revolutionary changes in our culture. These people believe kids should make their own rules. Let the results of their parenting speak. It will!

Our world is a world in which mistakes happen and moral standards are broken. Therefore, in an imperfect world, forgiveness and repentance (changing our minds to the extent we change our lives) are needed to handle the problem of our imperfections and our guilt while the consequences of our actions are left intact. Forgiveness is the world that is promoted in its most livable and effective form in the Christian faith, which was once the foundation of Western society. We have a God who forgives, even when we don't deserve it, and who loves us, even if we don't deserve it, making a new start possible for imperfect beings.

An amoral world, however, implodes. A moral world looks for real forgiveness from others who are also imperfect and in need of forgiveness, too. In the case of the Christian faith, the model for forgiveness comes from God. Would you like to live in this kind of world?

We Can Create Who We Are — Identity Dismantled Is In the Mind

Do you have a child or teen who is toying with the idea of becoming another gender? Some applications to higher learning institutions provide the opportunity for the student to choose any of 87 different genders (crazy!), and especially to choose the opposite of the two scientifically known genders, male or female. According to postmodernist thought, we can change identities as often as we like. To them, human nature is not a reality; it is a myth. Nothing makes us who we are; we make ourselves. Where do we see evidence for this anywhere in the real world? This is akin to the myths of ancient Greek mythology, and even less realistic. All living creatures have a nature unique to their kind, and that includes male and female natures. A lot of other features are also part of these natures.

Can we change our gender identities at will? Of course not. If we are male or female, our
chromosomes will always be what we were born with. So to put it bluntly, to claim we are a female when we were born a male (or vice-versa) is to lie to ourselves in the face of the real and unchangeable facts. A change of gender is all in the mind and beliefs, certainly not a physical reality.

But why does our postmodern culture accept as real something that isn't real? Because they want us to believe there are no universal truths, not even truths about our identities. And also because they have borrowed from Nietzsche the crazy idea that there are "no facts only, interpretations."[6] To make this clear postmodernists declare there are no objective realities and no objective facts. Can you believe such absurdity? Objective truths, such as scientific truths (facts) or historical truths (facts), are not facts. They are not real! As you can imagine, these claims have got them into hot water with the scientific community. Denying the reality of the Holocaust is a historical case in point that only underlines the crooked thinking embedded in such statements. These thoughts are failed mutations of the thinking of European philosophers whose ideas have more than once failed to take our real world into account. Why would any philosophy do that?

In order to avoid obvious criticism, they also declare reason and logic are not legitimate tools of thinking or criticism. They pose, supposedly protected in their ivory towers from all logical attacks and the inevitable forces of common sense — or so they think. If you ask why would anyone believe or teach these unreasonable ideas, we can only say, it is beyond us.

---

[6] I was reading today a quote from a noted professor who hailed Nietzsche as, "... the great 19th-century philosopher." Such is the about turn in the evaluation of him in our day. Nietzsche made some of the most irrational and crooked statements of all of the 19th-century philosophers. However, his negative influence on philosophy has been immeasurable due to his famous rant, "God is dead," a saying that many philosophers have happily rallied around. Come 1900 AD, it was reported, "Nietzsche is dead." A reading of his torrents of bitter diatribe against his favorite targets, Christianity and morals, are hard to endure or even believe they came from an educated man. Some worship his writings; others regard his life as interesting case material. He resigned nine years after he became a full professor and ten years later, he become insane.

Follow Your Heart! Forgetting Your Head?

Another concern from which parents must protect their children (by the use of sound reason and common sense) is the belief that has infiltrated our culture in the form of the postmodernist claim that feelings are more important to follow than reason. Well, as you have noticed, postmodernists have shrewdly shunned all reason and logic in the popular phrase "follow your heart." Emotions have mounted the throne.

There are some situations in which emotions are to be followed, so there is some truth in the statement "follow your heart." But let's hope that even in the choice of a lifelong mate, rationality is allowed a seat at our mental table along with our emotions. In fact, we should hear from both head and heart and give both their needed voice. If a person decides to follow their heart, it should be after they have duly consulted their reason.

The popularity of these postmodern ways of speaking and thinking in a world that has already shifted to a wide acceptability of uninhibited moral behavior should be clear to all parents. However, we must concede that responsible and truthful behavior are not always popular. Hence, the specious use of political correctness. Parents are having to fight this "freedom culture," which is turning out to be a very controlling culture. We are, perhaps, getting a sense of how important this culture is. Even primitive cultures recognize the importance of guarding their culture.

Be Your Own Psychologist

"All aspects of psychology (human behavior) are to be individually determined" is yet another idea of this new way of thinking. If I am told I have acted meanly, it is my decision as to whether I am mean, not someone else's. There are no set rules or laws that can say I am mean. I am my own psychologist. Simply put, if I don't think I was mean, I wasn't, and that ends the matter.

Another way of putting it is, everyone can do "what is right in their own eyes" and no one can, nor should, condemn them. This is called "being totally free and enjoying the absolute freedom, which is everyone's right" — free from judgment and criticism, too. No one is to be judged is the popular appeal of this point of view. Now, that's an astounding radical rewriting of culture. Historically, no culture has ever existed for long in which the absence of judgment of any sort was encouraged or imposed. If it did exist, it would mean no one could point out the wrong behavior of others, even if it were to their benefit to do so. Postmodernism is the first cultural revolution that has been this deviant. Common sense says it won't work as a culture, and this hypersensitivity to criticism for all humans is a fall into immaturity, not a rise to maturity.

Common sense would ask, "What happens when everyone does what is right in their own eyes?" Answer: no one has ever lived this way without finding themselves clashing fatally with others. Even Confucius said, "Don't do to others what you would not want done to yourself." Jesus bettered it by making it not just a standard for negative behavior but for positive behavior as well: "Do to others what you would have them to do to you." This is the beginning of a workable psychology.

Western psychology has been opposed to doing what is right in our own eyes. Restraint makes a peaceful society possible. Doing what is right in our own eyes is the path to inconsiderate acts of all sorts and, eventually, to war. Postmodernism prides itself on selling its cultural radicalism on showing tolerance, kindness, and consideration for others (not all, however) when, in fact, it creates the opposite. It should not advocate being your own psychologist when that makes the individual the sovereign judge of their own behavior. Such a principle is not considerate of others, nor open to their legitimate criticisms. Sensitivity can be a weakness if it is self-centered and, not surprisingly, it creates an insensitivity to others. Nor should we hide from the truth, unless we are afraid of the truth. As Paul put it, "Speak the truth in love." Speak it; don't not speak it. However, he says, love is the medium in which truth is to be conveyed — a word to the wise parent.

Entitlement — A Red Light!

If your child is demanding their rights and showing signs of a growing entitlement, a red flag is waving in your face. Add up the postmodernist beliefs and they encourage a person to insist on their rights, live in a dreamworld of absolute freedom, and expect to have their problems solved by other people. Entitlement results in forgetting our responsibility to others and to failing to build a workable, loving society. It creates a world of dependency rather than human achievement, a world where blame is the currency of its failings. Entitlement is the opposite of personal responsibility and of seeing the need for earning our way in life. It creates expectations that my needs should be met, and must be met, even if I am not attempting to be the source of their provision.

I was fortunate to be born into a pioneering country and was taught from the beginning that if I wanted something, I had to make it or earn it. No able-bodied or able-minded person had a free ride. Gifts were an act of love, not a way of life. Depending on others was a disgrace to society. If able, everyone should live for the betterment of others, because in that is the real fulfillment of our life on earth.

Today, parents often find themselves in a bind. If they don't provide what their child feels entitled to, the child threatens to leave, or the parent fears this possibility. Fear then becomes the motivation behind many a parental action and children are quick to smell the advantage to them.

The way of thinking that needs to be changed and taught early in life is: (1) There is pride in achieving things on our own. (2) We are here as much to help others as to enjoy life ourselves. You will find me quoting repeatedly, "Do to others as you would have them do to you." Both of the above points, when lived as our creed, create for us a high self-esteem. This high self-esteem has been undermined by the postmodern way of thinking, which amounts to a self-centered and selfish individualism that degrades our senses of worth. Keep telling your child it is better to feel proud of what they do than to get mad when others don't do what they feel others should do for them.

Straight thinking has been adulterated by half-truths and devious argumentation, intentionally trying to deceive and resulting in the proliferation of lies. Half-truths are the breeding ground of entitlement. The half that has appeal is used as bait to catch the unthinking victim.

In short, the areas in which this thinking has penetrated and changed our culture are: anti-truth, subjectivity, anti-rationalism, social justice, feelings, diversity, pluralism, gender, cultural flattening, anti-meganarratives, anti-patriotism, anti-capitalism, anti-rationality, and (in a big way) deceptive politics, of course.

News Flash! The Twentieth Century, The Bloodiest Yet — Why?

Could it be because of the faulty and divisive world views that the twentieth century has produced that it was stamped with such infamy? Just think of Stalin, Hitler, and the ideologies they militantly promoted. History has recorded their thinking that produced the bigotry, hatred, and unspeakable blood-stained cruelty of their actions.

Don't overlook the fact that it was also in the twentieth century that Postmodernism's way of thinking was born. If it is argued that it was born to combat the demons of hate that the twentieth century witnessed, it has failed miserably. It has, itself, fueled for the people of the twenty-first century more division, bigotry, hatred, and even bloodshed — the inevitable fruit of its intolerant beliefs, dressed in sophistry and spread in the name of tolerance, of all things. It had only one thing right: twist the minds of people and their behavior follows in kind.

Crooked Thinking, the Enemy of Truth

Crooked thinking never arrives at the truth. Crooked thinking is also an unintelligent way of trying to demolish the truth. Students often do not recognize the crooked thinking that, at times, is the tool used to convince them of fallacious ideas. The itinerant teachers that walked from town to town in early Greece taught the skills of sophistry, what is seen today as intelligent reshaping of the facts.

Many of us absorb crooked thinking by osmosis, similar to the way we pick up the infection of the virus called COVUD-19. Parents can fail to talk about the faulty thinking that is prevalent in the world around them and, as a result, their children more easily become mentally infected by other ideas. We must understand, all thinking is not "straight" and straight thinking is taught, not caught.

Correct the Real Cause

What is the cause of all this crooked thinking? It's no surprise. A new way of thinking has been thrust on us by the untested, crooked thinking and mental meanderings of philosophers. And now it's what people, most of them unwittingly, have come to think and accept as the inevitable culture of our day. It's something the ordinary person feels helpless to combat. Yes, most people tolerate some of its results, while its subtle beginnings in the life of universities has become subtle no longer. Students, taught by the universities to think like postmodernists, turn around and insist the university do as they think, and the university succumbs to their demands. It has permeated all walks of life. Politicians have succumbed to its possible paths to power. (It has become a dominant power play in dishonest politics today, with little concern for ethical standards).

It has a name: Postmodernism, supported by materialism and the theory of natural selection. Even churches (whose pastors are, in some cases, trained by theologians who proudly claim they are postmodernists to one degree or another) have bowed to its unrelenting call to accept its invasion of culture in order to be "relevant." The struggle is between relevancy and truth.

Universities are the seedbed of this cultural revolution. Academic disciplines, such as English Composition (surprisingly), have replaced the reading of the classics with a baptism into the graphic, and yes, erotic liberation of the "stifled" traditional mind. A professor of English Composition in a state college subjected the students to a video of a male teenager demonstrating how to masturbate. This is preferred English Composition? You judge the intent of this professor's choice of material. Only the hard sciences are largely free from postmodernist influence, except where personal opinion has wrongly injected itself. The social sciences and schools of the arts have become, in most universities, expressions of postmodernist thought. Postmodernism has now become the accepted philosophy of our age in many academic strongholds. If you want to know what it teaches, it is not too much to say, "Just observe the culture in which we are living." The shift has been revolutionary and, to tell you the truth, a new "revolution" is the goal of those who have gained influence over our minds. I say "minds" because that is where revolution lives and propagates.

Has this cause affected teens and adults as well as children? You know the answer to that. The interesting thing is, it came to the USA from Europe and was led by French Parisian proponents. Violence on both continents, which is not confined to any one country, is being practiced by its more extreme exponents, who want to destroy all meganarratives and follow, literally, its teachings.

Unlimited freedom, entitlement, and the death of truth as we have known it are among the beliefs that have restructured how people think. Fertile and destructive offshoots and behaviors are among the practical fruits of this foolish philosophy.

The education of our children and youth has been one of the main tools for transforming our culture and hence, my opening reference to parents who now find themselves on the front line of cultural change. It is to help parents in any way I can that I offer tools for a successful counter struggle. If you are, maybe unknowingly, convinced that the new culture is an improvement, I ask you to keep an open mind and read further to evaluate the results.

News flash! The philosophy of Postmodernism has run its course because of its false, unrealistic claims and self-refutation. The culture, however, is going to take some time to run its course, as history has taught us repeatedly. Culture changes more slowly as people are slowly made aware of its deceptions and problems. The benefits to parents who struggle on the front line to bring about change are great, if we accept the challenge.

Students must also think for themselves and get an understanding of what the postmodernist educational influences are and how to detect the mental bias. They are beliefs, just like your parent's ideas are their beliefs. That they are not the best way to think or live your life, this we tend to find out too late. If what you are being taught is not the way the teacher consistently lives outside of class, then don't swallow his/her principles. Something is wrong or missing. One of the questions to ask the professor is, "Do you consistently live by these principles in your every day life? For example, do you live as though there are no objective truths or universal truths?" Then watch to see if his answer is honest. Does he act as though all reality is not real? You can notice if he chooses the doorway instead of the wall to walk out of the building. Does he act as though the law of gravity (a universal and objective truth) is real or not? Does he drive on the left or right side of the road? You get the picture?

Teaching Tools

For Teaching Straight Thinking and Avoiding Crooked Thinking

Tools for parents to combat some of the issues that have been discussed in this chapter occur in the following chapters. The tools I offer here are for teaching straight thinking to our youth and to combat crooked thinking. Start with these.

Here's how and what to teach:

Responsibility

Parents must accept the responsibility of educating their children on how to think. How to think straight is not something we are born with. We need to learn it. Our mental system is, as far as we know, the most complicated system in the universe and its skilled use is a matter of education.

Don't leave that education to the schools because they seldom, if ever, systematically and consistently teach it. Parents fill a place of great influence in their children's lives. We are to use our minds as our intelligent designer intended them to be used. They are both inspectors of the accuracy of what we see, hear, taste, touch, and smell, and a judge of its value. You are your own private investigator. Impart the wisdom of how to use our minds effectively and accurately and you will have trained good and straight thinkers.

Determined Mindset

This task will not be effectively completed if we don't have a mind that is set firmly on the importance of the task. Begin each day with it in your mind and don't end the day without having satisfactorily completed it for that day to your satisfaction.

Here's the Framework for Your Task.

Repeatedly teach and use the following methods:

- Ask questions of what they see, hear, taste, touch, and smell — but not about everything. Don't kill the intrigue and interest they might have by over-emphasizing.

- You can ask what, how, why, where, and when about nature, human nature, thoughts, ideas, and all the products of the mind — and always for the purpose of noting the wonder of our world and its intelligent, purposeful, design.

- Questions are not the only lead into nature's wonders. Comments, your personal points of view, discussions, and searching the web with them are all good starting points. Train them to "use the eyes of their mind" — not just their physical eyes — and listen with the ears of their mind, too.

- All tools for developing the family's skills should be used often, since the brain learns best by repetition. What is repeatedly learned and practiced becomes a strong circuit in the brain and, therefore, increases the likelihood that the person will resort to them, use them, and see their wisdom.

- All tools should be delivered in a calm spirit — without triggering the emotions of the child, thus causing anger and resistance. Love is the most excellent medium for opening the mind and stimulating a receptive mood. Rule of thumb: speak the truth in a loving way that is obvious to your child.

- When using these tools, do not begin with a negative rebuke but with the positive example of how to think correctly.

Teach the Following Points

Reject…

- What contradicts what we know to be true of our world, such as that our world and all that is in it is reality to which we must pay attention and not act as though it is not there or is not happening.

- Whatever is other than common sense: what makes common sense is to be preferred over any other sense. Whatever is contradictory to common sense: common sense is the sense that has been accepted as true over the many centuries of known human experience. Example: Love is better than hate. Don't accept anything that denies this fact. Rule of thumb: "If the obvious sense makes common sense, accept no other sense."

- What contradicts itself: To state something that contradicts another of your own statements is to blatantly commit a logical error. This is one of the litmus tests for straight thinking. Self-refutation ("shooting yourself in the foot") will not lead to the truth, nor to people thinking you are intelligent.

- Contradictions: Train your children to spot contradictions. Play games, spotting contradictions. Use the news, or some movie, or a passage from a book or an article, or anything that gives you the opportunity to see who spots the first contradiction. Example: To say, "There is no truth that applies to everyone," contradicts itself because it is implied there is one truth that applies to everyone — namely, "there is no truth that applies to everyone." It contradicts its own claim. It disagrees with itself. It is self-refuting. Outright contradictions are easier to detect than this subtle error.

- What demeans who we are: Humans can't live happily when they think they are not worth anything, nor can they settle for what robs them of the desire to live. Teach that we must always settle for what gives us the greatest sense of worth and dignity. The beliefs of Christianity do exactly this.

- What does not consider all the facts, or excludes some facts so that it can make its point: This is a common mistake. Always ask, "Are there other facts that are not being taken into account that contradict this conclusion?"

These points are commonly made in postmodernist thinking, which is re-shaping our culture.

Use the following definition of straight and crooked thinking and discuss each with your children. You are the teacher.

Straight Thinking
If we are going to have a belief built on evidence, we will need straight thinking. Example: I believe the world is round. What evidence of that do we have?

Straight thinking is thinking:

- Factually (which means with all the facts fairly represented).

- Accurately (which means telling the whole truth and nothing but the truth about all the facts, not just some of the facts as is often done when the arguments are specious). Arguments that have the ring of truth but are, in reality, misleading are the stock in trade of modern day sophists.

- Truthfully (which means without falsification and twisting of the facts).

- Honestly (which includes being motivated by honesty as well as being honest). An honest basis for reasoning starts in the heart, in our love for others.

- Representing reality (not building a case on speculation, fantasy, or imagination and then passing it off as truth).

- Verifiably (meaning using facts that can be evidentially verified). Evidence is found in our physical universe (including all the minutest details of living creatures) and in our valid experiences, not forgetting our subjective realities.

- Consistently (meaning without contradiction or flipping your position, like politicians often do). Presenting your reasons without changing them in midstream to avoid being trapped. This consistency is the bread and butter of a solid argument.

- Unadulterated by irrelevant facts (means don't divert from the point being discussed by changing the discussion to facts that are not relevant). Don't chase irrelevant rabbits so that the discussion is diverted to trivial details.

- Justly (meaning what is fair and impartial).

- Logically (what we will call straight thinking and the opposite of crooked thinking). Logical thinking is thinking from accurate and defensible assumptions, then constructing logically rational arguments based upon your assumption. Of this, you will find plenty of examples in this book. If you need to, you will learn straight thinking as you read.

Unfortunately, the way of thinking that lay behind the latest changes to our culture fails on all these counts. Postmodernism and its accepted theories — materialism and natural selection — are a classic example of trampling all over straight and logical thinking[7].

Crooked Thinking

We use crooked thinking when our thinking is inaccurate, dishonest, or crooked, and when we say or do any or all of the following:

- Saying, "Everyone thinks this," when everyone doesn't; or "Everyone does it," when everyone doesn't (an argument parents are familiar with), or "We all know this to be a fact," when it is not universally believed. This is called stretching the truth, exaggeration, and sometimes, blatant lying in the hope no one will fact check us. When citing common sense, it is a valid argument only if those listening to you agree that it is commonly held to be sensible.

---

[7] A discussion and exposure of postmodernist thinking, along with a further elucidation of straight and crooked thinking will be found in the author's blog.

- Fastening on a trivial point in the discussion while avoiding the main issue. Declaring the whole argument to be false because a minor divergence from accuracy is observed.

- In formal argument, arguing that a dubious point is universally accepted, when in fact, it isn't universally accepted.

- Resorting to illogical reasoning that is based on false assumptions. This invalidates the whole argument. The assumption must be restated accurately and the reasoning must possess the ability to support the restated assumption.

- Manipulating people's emotions by making shocking statements that cannot be defended or do not represent the whole truth in order to get people to believe what is being argued. Because emotions are usually a part of an argument, they must not be given more importance than the emotions should rightly have.

- Using one's education or status to claim validity for ones own statements. This is hiding behind status or education and asking to be believed.

To sharpen your own thinking, think of examples of each of the above and use them in the mental training of your children. Teaching is often the way for parents to learn best.

Choose examples that are age appropriate. Be a parent who takes seriously the training of their own mind and a parent who also takes seriously the development of their children's minds.

3 — The Watershed

A watershed is a dramatic divide. Standing at the top of Hoosier Pass, which crosses the continental divide in Colorado, the point is driven home. Water that falls inches apart will end up opposite coasts — either in the Pacific or Atlantic oceans, and the twain shall never meet again before they leave this continent. The divide in ideas and beliefs are just as precise as the divide at the summit of the Continental Divide. Lean one way just a little and the destination is the opposite of leaning a little the other way.

A great divide in the thinking of our Western culture has occurred in the last 400 years, and this divide is even more dramatic. Several factors were the cause of this divide. The fever over the differences hasn't ended yet, and the tables are turning in favor of what was popularly believed by most people over 400 years ago. Along with the original parting of the ways, there are multiple effects that have shaped our culture.

You are no doubt aware of how the beliefs in our Western culture have changed over the last 2,000 years or so, but especially at warp speed in the last 50 years. Each new wave of teenagers is forming their own beliefs and with them, creating their own "in vogue" lingo. Emojis are now part of our language. "You" is spelled "u," and "u" should recognize "LOL." Technology is advancing fast, and underlying it are the changes in beliefs that parents are facing in their children's new ways of thinking. Change always begins in the mind — with our thinking.

Change is, however, not always good. It can be upsetting, unnerving, and challenge a love of permanence, regularity, and continuity. Parents are aching for more of this trilogy. One thing is for certain: our teens' latest beliefs will keep parents on edge as their children surf the net and bring home ideas that, at times, are a shock. As a result, some parents just sink into worry. Others show symptoms akin to PTSD!

"Last year my teen was a confirmed believer in God and now, after only a few months, she is a militant atheist, or so it seems. What do I do? I see signs of her becoming a Taoist, whatever that is. And after the school's sexual education classes, I see her drawing away from me and her obvious changes in behavior keep me awake at night," worried one distressed parent. Variety (change), we are told, is the spice of life. Or in the speed of this fast-moving culture, has it become life's habanero sauce? You will need, first, to know where the really important divide in the way people think is — its exact location. Beliefs inches apart will end up in opposite directions.

Are parents required to answer all questions? And if so, which ones? Philosophy will tell you: start with the big ones. They are the ones causing the great divide of thought and belief. More precisely, the biggest one is THE question that formed the watershed in the first place: God or no God; which? And that question affects many other big questions, such as "Who am I?" and "How should I live?" Questions like these are currently in a state of flux because Postmodernism says there is no such thing as human nature (Really?), as well as denying God's nature, of course (God is, by nature, spirit). It teaches that the identity of our nature can change whenever and to whatever we choose. Is your teen showing signs of wanting to change genders? Some other major questions that form the framework of our thinking are: How did the

world originate? Does it matter which religion I choose?
What happens when we die? (Many children ask that one).

The fundamental question that changes the way we think
about all these big questions is "God or no God." It has, to all
intents and purpose, for many scientists, higher education
teachers, and professors, been long settled — but not for all
of them. The debate is still a current discussion, believe it or
not. However, all attempts are being made to sideline it. You
know the routine: if you can't get rid of it, marginalize it.
Parents, as we shall see, can't afford to stand by and shrug
their shoulders. The minds of their children are at stake.

So, in which direction will we find satisfying answers to all
these questions? That depends on the answer to the first big
question, the watershed! Parents will need to address this
often as their child's understanding and knowledge increases
and changes in their beliefs are becoming more evident.

The Great Divide In the History of Thought
Our answer to the question "God or no God" will lead us in
opposite directions, east or west, directions that will have very
different results in our lives. What affects everything in our
lives starts in our minds, remember!

The loss of certainty (which resulted from a revolt against the
idea of God, a belief in whom had kept culture on an even
keel for centuries) started in earnest around 1600 AD.
Descartes believed in God. Belief in God was the immovable
rock in the culture of his day. However, he started to think
without including the firmly believed reality of God. His ideas
ended up favoring doubt, not faith — or not a faith in God.
His final belief, after his mental meanderings, was that truth
rested in the individual consciousness of man. Effectively, he

had relegated God to the back seat of life's theatre. The great divide in philosophic thought had been seriously revealed.

The divide soon became a threatening problem, and it was in the rise of scientific optimism that the paths started to sharply diverge. Science initially grew up in the lap of the church, so to speak, but both became uncomfortable with each other. Science was based on a materialistic philosophy, and the church continued on the path of a theistic belief. Although the philosophy that formed the foundation of scientific endeavors did not explicitly exclude God, it did not include him, either. The biggest question of all, "Is there a God?", was being demoted in the minds of many, and in the endeavors of science, to a position of lesser importance or of none at all. The day would soon come when the full focus of the philosophy that directed science would be on a belief in a naturalistic and materialistic world, excluding all that was not matter. Since God was apparently not matter, he was on the way out. Spirit was questioned.

God was now clearly a side issue, if he was considered at all. "God is dead!" wrote Nietzsche in the late nineteenth century. His declaration could have been easily forecasted. It would have caused a huge stir if it had been made 300 years earlier. But it met in the nineteenth century with mostly little comment. It was now not earth shattering news for many people. Soon, the thinking within the church — namely, in the "Death of God School" — would follow suit and the watershed saw the unexpected.

In theological circles, the idea of the death of God was publicly received without the earthquake it should have created. A twist to the beliefs of the "Death of God school" appeared in John Robinson's book *Honest to God*, where he simply sought to rewrite who God was in a manner that would be acceptable to the growing naturalistic view of the world around him. "Our image of God must go," he wrote. As Bishop of Woolwich, he had considerable influence and whereas the church had sought to win people to Christ by repentance and faith, it was clearly not the road the *new theology* was going to take in the future.

No philosophers began with discussing the idea of a God, either. Whether you believed in a personal God or not was now becoming a purely subjective issue, a matter of the heart, not of the head. In the fields of higher learning, it was either rejected or patronized as an issue for the heart to decide. The head knew better.

Science came, perhaps unwittingly, to the rescue. Design in nature and in the universe is now an undeniable fact. The observation of design everywhere has now opened the discussion around the question, "Can you have design without a designer?" Science is not jumping to accept the idea of a designer, even though it is the most likely and logical answer. It is outside of the philosophy of science to consider a personal designer, especially because God seems to posses no physical substance that can be examined. So where are we now?

Faith and Belief

The story of thought is the story of philosophy, which is the story of beliefs. Faith is another word for our beliefs. If God is only a subjective issue — a personal option, a matter for faith alone, a retreat to something that comforts many when the going is rough — then why is it faith and the need for beliefs have never left the front seats of human experience? Because all humans must believe something — have some kind of faith? Yes, but let's ask it again as it is being asked

49

today: In this "enlightened" world, can't we get rid of the need for faith along with the need for God? The answer is no, because it is an essential manner in which people function. Beliefs are the wells from which our actions spring. We never act without a belief of some sort. The total human mental system would have to be reconstructed to do away with the need for faith (beliefs).

Atheist Richard Dawkins (author of 105 books), in his most popular book *The God Delusion,* finds the need to do battle with this observable reality. He struggles. Faith is in us all. The atheist has a faith — a belief — and cannot deny it. Dawkins also acknowledges the inherent faith of children in what appears to him to be a biological predisposition to believe in God, even to believe in him as the creator of the heavens and the earth — "God forbid!" In another of his books *The Roots of Religion,* he settles with an intellectual sleight of hand that for him explains this "evolutionary blunder." The atheist has to blame something, so evolution must have goofed, he suggests. What a confession! And he must have felt the barb of truth as his thoughts raced and trembled over his confession.

Remember the children's hymn that challenges Dawkins' apparent evolutionary blunder:

> "All things bright and beautiful,
> All creatures great and small,
> All things wise and wonderful,
> The Lord God made them all."

It's part of an undying biological predisposition to believe in a creator God, according to Dawkins — also, according to the remembered experiences of billions of us.

Why do humans seem primed to believe in God and need to cling to some faith — something to believe in — whatever their age? It's not a silly question. It is a question about a reality of life that humans have known from the earliest days of their time on earth and intuited from their earliest age. We can't eradicate an innate human urge or a functional need for belief to play an essential part in the way we are made to function. Nor can we remove a felt need for some greater authority to whom we can turn.

All humans operate with a faith in something. Why? Because faith will always be "the substance of things hoped for." It's human to believe and to feel the sweetness of hope. We all do it everyday. Even atheists find the need to believe something, and they become militant about their beliefs, thereby acknowledging belief's importance to all of us. So, getting rid of faith would not be the next step of choice for those who have already walked away from God at the watershed.

The Search for an Alternative to Belief in God

Two things more were needed for humanistic philosophy to maintain its dominancy and for God to be convincingly sidelined, quieting the pestering tinges of doubt in the minds of those who wanted to remove him from consideration. First, because the philosophers of this persuasion were not willing to accept God as the creator of what was obviously an amazing world — beyond the ability of humans to create, or even conceive in their wildest dreams — they needed an alternative explanation of how the world had come to be.

Darwin came to the rescue, and the theory of evolution by means of natural selection was received with great relief and uncritical acclaim. It was believed to the point of allegedly being a proven law of nature, which was the overly optimistic reception given to it by those who were desperate for an alternative to an intelligent designer.

Now, with the rise of evolutionary theory, it was believed we could do away with the idea of a creator God, and not look back. However, look back we must, because there is a challenge that will deal a fatal blow to evolution in the minds of all those who will be open to its obvious truth. A workable essential design requires an intelligent designer. This is inescapable.

The Death of Truth

The second thing that was astutely seen as necessary by the first authors of Postmodernism was to engineer the death of absolute truth. If only they could engineer the death of God and the death of truth, the minds of the world would be in their grasp. Once this was done, the path at the watershed that led away from God would feel safe for all "reasonable" people to negotiate. Why would it feel safe? Because no longer would there be any universal truth, any universal belief in any thing absolute. All that was left would be something subjective — personal opinion to believe in God — if people so foolishly and unnecessarily chose.

The Methodology of Postmodernism

All that was needed now was a methodology to accomplish this end. Postmodernism has done this with the aid of all the humanistic philosophies before it that accepted a materialistic and humanistic way of thinking about everything. The methodology was to cunningly change the way people think by changing the way the culture thought. The change in the culture could be engineered via an insistence on absolute freedom for everyone, where truth became entirely a personal issue, making it possible to say, "That may be true for you, but it isn't true for me," and the statement would go unchallenged. Truth, now, would be nothing more than a person's own perception of things. This they have largely achieved in the fields of education, entertainment, the arts, and politics, and in almost all of our current culture. Postmodernism has made it happen by astutely changing the *thinking of the young* and patiently waiting for the young to "infect" the next generation. Observe how that has happened since around 1970 AD.

We are now fighting for the re-establishment of objective, universal, absolute truth in the minds and culture of our day. The maxim, "There is no such thing as absolute truth," has been rashly welcomed because it came wrapped in the attractive package of absolute freedom for everyone (even though it was not said that a greater control over our lives was the real nature of this deceptive packaging). We can once again raise the flag of real hope and truth and defeat this way of thinking in the minds of all who will listen, because there is a fatal and obvious flaw(s) in Postmodernism's thinking about truth and freedom, which results in illogical, unreasonable, and plainly false statements.

The paths to self knowledge (Who am I?), as well as to the other big questions of life, diverge and will charge in opposite directions over the question of "God or no God" and "truth or no absolute truth." You will discover many reasons in this book why your belief in God's existence will shape how and what you think about yourself, your world, and how you will choose to live. We all will need to have a belief founded in a personal conviction if it is going to be efficacious.

Remember, we saw in *Compelling Evidence for God* that the evidence we can observe in our universe points overwhelmingly to the existence of an intelligent source who designed the entire universe with clear purpose. Intelligence, purpose, and design are written everywhere for all to see. They cannot be denied! Even atheists do not deny the evidence of design. At the very least, we have to accept that we are intelligently and purposefully designed creatures. This evidence is where we start when answering the questions "God or no God?", "Who or what am I?", and "How should we live?" [At this point, you may wish to refresh your minds with a reread of *Compelling Evidence for God.*]

We will not get far with helping our children if we don't settle our own beliefs, first. Then, and only then, can we effectively help our children settle theirs. They, too, need to have a faith settled in both the head and the heart. The "craziness of things like Postmodernism," as Noam Chomsky put it, should make us relegate it to the rubbish heap. I suggest Hume's advice that he offered for something unrelated to postmodernism: "To the flames!" I can't think of a more suitable comment regarding the worth of Postmodernist's ridiculous and damaging beliefs.

The Counter Argument
(Set Out in Detail in 1809)

The evidence for design in our universe is so obvious that it doesn't need advanced microscopes and telescopes to be seen. However, these tools have, in the skilled hands of scientists, simply shown us so much more. The words of the Apostle Paul, written before these tools where even dreamed of, sums up what is obvious to all of us in a profound statement.

> *For since the creation of the world, God's invisible qualities, his eternal power and divine nature — have been clearly seen, being understood from what has been made, so that men are without excuse,*[8]

In 1809, Dr William Paley DD wrote a book that is regarded as a classic. It compiled in detail the knowledge available in his day that led to an argument for intelligent design. It was published in 1860 and was still regarded as worth re-publishing in 2012. His argument has not been refuted, nor has it lost any of its power.

As evidence has been further accumulated by the much more detailed scientific findings of our day in bio-chemistry and physics, plus other scientific disciplines, and aided by the amazing advances in scientific equipment and the scientists' own skills, Paley's argument has been confirmed. The words of Paul have also been further verified. The old-standing argument for an intelligent universe, filled with intelligently designed creatures and organisms, is stronger than ever.

This argument, based on the clear evidence supporting a purposefully designed universe and the inevitable rationality of an intelligent designer — Paley's argument — is more than worth our recounting. Let's follow his argument. I will transform the antiquated English into the parlance of today, as needed, and abbreviate to save us pages of, at times, difficult reading. You can read it for yourself in the reprint of his book,

---

[8] Romans 1:20.

Natural Theology, reprinted in 2012, and easily obtainable, if you desire.

> *When crossing a heath (a somewhat barren and poorly drained open field) you happened to kick your foot against a stone. You could easily argue it had laid there forever. It would not be easy to dispute this conclusion and show it was in any sense absurd. But suppose you also stumbled on a watch lying on the ground. You would hardly conclude that it had laid there forever. Why would you not assume the same for the watch as for the stone? Because upon examination, the watch shows evidence of being purposefully designed, and recently in human history.*

[Paley's comparison of the stone and the watch are not totally valid since the stone can also be evidence of a purposeful design, just not as obvious to the people of his day. Paley's argument loses none of its validity, however. He goes on to explain the watch's intersecting parts, its choice of different materials: bronze and steel, etc. It has, he reminds us, a discoverable purpose: namely, to tell time. You would notice that if the mechanism's parts were even slightly off, it would not serve its purpose. The inference, he concludes, is inevitable — the watch must have had a maker or makers. The maker must have formed it for this purpose, understood its construction, and designed its use. Anybody would come to that conclusion.]

He continues... (My comments are in brackets following each point).

1. *This conclusion is not weakened by the fact that you may never have met a watchmaker with the ability to accomplish this result, or known of such a maker, or seen a watch being made, or even dreamed of the ability, let alone the actuality, of being able to make one yourself. The conclusion is not weakened by the fact that you could not conceive or engineer its design, or understand fully the laws that make it work. Your incredibility at the existence of such an ingenious device may be a stumbling block to your accepting it, but the conclusion would be inevitable. It does not weaken the argument if some existing materials were found nearby that had been used to make some or all of its parts. Nor does the time, place, or any other unknown factor affect in any way the conclusion that such a maker must have existed. [He adds one more inference.] It would not matter whether the maker were human, a different species, or have a different nature in some way from ours. The conclusion remains inevitable.*

    [If you struggle with God being the designer of the universe because you have never "met" him, your struggle does not weaken the evidence or the argument that he existed.]

2. Paley argues, *…nor would it invalidate the conclusion if the watch sometimes went wrong or needed adjustments from time to time. It would not matter whether we could account for these irregularities or not. Perfection of operation under all conditions is not essential to prove that it was designed. The watch*

clearly shows evidence of intelligent design, and that
cannot be discounted.

[Nature does not always perform in varying climatic
conditions, for example, with the same results.
Imperfection, therefore, does not weaken the evidence
or the fact of intelligent design in nature.]

3. *Nor would it matter if we did not understand the need*
   for some of the parts or had no knowledge as yet, of
   their purpose. The more complex the object, the more
   likely we would not be able to explain or understand its
   composition. Even if some parts seemed to be
   superfluous, the conclusion is not affected.

   [The macro and micro universe is beyond our
   understanding (we know so little), so that is not a
   reason to doubt the evidence we have. There is so
   much still to be discovered, more than can be
   accomplished in lifetimes ahead, if ever we could
   discover it all.]

4. *Nor is the conclusion affected if in the place where the*
   watch was found, substances were also found that
   were used in its creation.

   [Evolution seeks to hide behind this suggestion. Other
   substances could have been available at the time a
   next step in the evolutionary process was needed. So
   that, they say, explains the use of available
   substances. So what? The intelligent and purposeful
   design does not depend on explanations, or it is
   invalidated by them.]

5. *Nor would it make the conclusion more or less likely if a "principle of order" (a theory) existed that accounted for how the parts were arranged to achieve the watch's purpose or its design. It would also not affect the conclusion if there were no knowledge of how the principle that ordered its design worked (if any). Nor could the lack of understanding alter the conclusion. Nor if any intelligence distinct from the maker could be verified.*

[Likewise, none of these conditions affect the conclusion that the watch showed clear evidence of intelligent, purposeful design. Perhaps this point that Paley made is an answer to the philosophies of his age and those that keep popping up speculating on explanations, for example, of how reality is not real and is just in our minds. The belief that the obvious evidence of design was no proof of its design — simply a motivation to make us think so — does not alter the conclusion that common sense says there was a designer. "Reality is not real" is a statement of Postmodernism still in vogue some 211 years later. Paley's argument dispensed with it before it was thought of, so it cannot be used as a legitimate speculation to dispense with the reality of reality, or that the real universe has a designer.

All such unproven ideas of our age, or those gone by, can be seriously considered as negations of the evidence of intelligent, purposeful design.]

6. *It is a mistake to assign to any law an efficient operating cause of anything. A law presupposes an agent; it is not a cause. The law, be it a law of physics*

or any other law, is only the mode according to which the agent proceeds. Without the agent, the law does nothing. A law of nature cannot be assigned as the cause of anything while excluding the agent that uses it.

[The attempt to find a law that explains everything, such as "The Theory of Everything," does nothing to discover the cause of everything or anything.]

7. *Knowing nothing about how a watch operates or is made does not change the conclusion that it gives clear evidence of a purposeful designer. Our ignorance about the watch does not do away with what is obvious to our senses and our intelligence.*

[The argument that we don't know enough, yet, about our world is no counter to what is evidentially and overwhelmingly clear. If not knowing everything were a successful counter argument, then we probably will never know and the obvious evidence will go unaccounted for.]

At this point in Paley's argument, he introduces another, more convincing concept. Let's suppose that the watch reproduced itself. Let's say, after a while, it gave birth to a baby watch and the baby watch was nurtured by the watch we found and grew into an adult watch. Would this in any way change our conviction that the watch we found was purposefully designed by a maker?

Paley says, his admiration for the watch and the maker would only increase. I think that would be true for all who were not biased against allowing the evidence to impact them.

8. *The relationship of the found watch to the baby watch is not the same as the relationship of the found watch to its maker.*

[No comment needed.]

9. *What this discovery of reproduction would do is to make it less probable that the found watch came directly from the hand of the maker. The argument from design remains, however, as it was. There cannot be design without a designer, contrivance without a contriver, order without choice, arrangement without an arranger, a purpose without intention of purpose, without the end having ever been contemplated. The presence of intelligence and mind is only enhanced by other like designs*

[The objections often raised to this are in the form of "what we don't know invalidates what we do know" — false logic. Design necessitates a designer, especially a repeated design. Design is evidence of intelligence and repeated design, an impregnable barrier to doubt.]

10. *Nor does running back into the past indefinitely, watch after watch producing the subsequent watch, do away with the need for a maker, designer, and intelligence. It does not do away with the need for an original designer, period. The need for a maker is not diminished the further back we go. The conclusion is invincible: there was a maker, a designer, an intelligence that contrived with intended purpose, the watch.*

[An objection to this argument that is based on what we do not know about the past simply kicks the can down the road and is not evidence of any nature that invalidates the need of a designer for the watch.]

Can it be that the reproduction of one watch after another proves the opposite: namely, that no designer, maker, and intelligence is needed? This is absurdity! But as Paley adds, "Yet this is atheism."

Every indication of an intelligent designer for the watch that arises out of a careful study of it, also exists in nature, only more so — compellingly! The examples in nature are so many, they can't be counted. This remarkable scholar and scientist, whose works were required college courses for decades, covers in the ten points listed above, most of the hesitations and objections to believing in an intelligent, purposeful designer of this universe. The argument from design to designer is put beyond reasonable doubt, and that is why it has never been successfully refuted.

In the process, Paley identifies some of the invisible qualities that a designer of this universe must posses — intelligence, knowledge, power to create — and also makes a rational case for belief in a divine nature. All this points to a designer that has the qualities and attributes that are found in the biblical description of God! Coincidence? Or rational support for a belief in the biblical God? You must decide based on the evidence.

Paley and his argument have been subjected to intense vilification (a practice still in vogue today after 200 years). If you can't beat them, vilify them! So much for humankind becoming more civilized and tolerant as the years go by. Vilification of an author surely speaks to an obvious lack of available evidence with which to do the job and a lack of veracity on the part of the vilifier.

We have also understood that a belief in God or no God will always need to be settled beyond the evidence by a step of faith, convincingly fueled by the evidence. The need for a LEAP of faith, based on clear evidence of functional design, virtually proves the existence of a designer and the leap is growing smaller with the mounting scientific evidence we now possess. In fact, it is now beyond dispute for any fair-minded individual.

Faith will always be needed, because we cannot scientifically prove the existence of God, a being that has no physical substance. The ineffective use of a microscope, or telescope, or any of the amazing tools science has ingeniously invented, means God, by his non-material nature, has still avoided detection. God is spirit and exhibits the reality of a spirit being. Spirit is also part of the realities of life in this universe that we experience, and part of our human makeup. Science, then, can be a little frustrated, perhaps, that he lies beyond their ability to detect. We can't apply the facts of physics or any other tangibly limited scientific discipline to God for this reason. Even mathematics can't come to our aid. He is scientifically and in every way physically undetectable. Science has limited itself by its own philosophy, which insists there has to be a materialistic or naturalistic source and/or explanation for everything in our universe. God is beyond the reach of the materialistic scope of science. He is not beyond the detection of the human spirit and inner human experiences, however.

The only way we can find out tangibly about God and his existence is via the work of his hands, "the heavens and the earth" and all that is in them. The first chapter of the Bible points us to this wealth of evidence, and Paley sought to detail some of it for us. Therefore, we have been pointed to the evidence that we are urged to examine. Truth and right need never fear honest examination of evidence. Scientists have been hard at work, finding out all they can from what they study of our world. Our thanks to the scientists for their ingenious work. The question for all of us is, "What does 'the heavens and the earth' and all that is in them tell us?"

Richard Dawkins — Confused and Conflicted!

An interesting aside to all this are the conflicting statements of Richard Dawkins, who has been claimed as the leading exponent and defender of atheism and evolution today. After studying Paley's *Natural Theology,* he praised Paley and then proceeded to write his defense of atheism (more accurately a repudiation of there being a God) in his book *The Blind Watchmaker,* an obvious reference to Paley's illustration of the watch found out on the heath.

Dawkins offers the explanation that since design is so evident in nature and can't be denied, it must be only the *appearance* of a design, not an *actual* design. He then struggles in his book to be able to show that design can be only an appearance, not real or actual. However, the appearance of design is everywhere in the universe and in every cell of our own bodies. It is not only an appearance, because this appearance of design we find in nature functions the same as an actual design. Think of the blood stream, its vast reach into every cell of the body, and its effective conveyance of nutrients and disposal of waste. If not an actual design, what is it? An "appearance only" of a design will not meet the requirements of a functioning human system? An actual design will. If it is an appearance of design only, then appearances — in this case at least — are real, actual, and efficacious. Dawkins argument is crooked. It does not deal adequately with the facts.

A Direction for Everything

To believe God exists or does not exist are for both positions (theist and atheist), finally, an act of faith. The atheist's attempt to render faith a spurious, subjective action is self refuting. The experiential verification of whether or not we have read the evidence of the heavens and the earth correctly and have chosen the right belief will be seen in the kind of life our belief leads us to live — also, in the degree of fulfillment and happiness it gives us.

This is true for all of us, since all of us will take up, in essence, one of two positions: we believe there is a God, or we don't. "We don't know" amounts, practically, to the same as "we don't believe" there is a God. This is called agnosticism, where we sit on the fence, hanging on to the middle ground — namely, that we do not know or can't make up our minds. This supposed neutral position does not cancel out the possibility of God's existence either. So, practically, it is a choice for all of us between God or no God. God wants our trust so that a relationship can be built. Note: "I don't know; I am an agnostic" eliminates effective trust.

Let's set out the facts for a belief in God to ascertain the direction our beliefs will lead us.

• Scientific proof or disproof either way of a physically undetectable being is not possible. Therefore, any belief about God calls for faith and an examination of available evidence.

- The evidence we find in the "heavens and the earth" and all that is in it provides the only "tangible proof" we can obtain. Do we need more? It is already compelling to the fair judgment of an open mind. Remember Paul's argument in Romans 1:20 that I quoted above.

- The Bible claims to be a revelation from God, and we can examine in its pages the life a faith in God provides. We can also experience the spiritual and psychological results of our own faith if we live trusting him.

- Additionally, we can examine the lives of consistent followers of atheism. (Have there been any, or do they all steal a little from what God says is the way life works best?) Moral truths, such as "Do to others as you would have them do to you," are among the most common thefts that atheists appropriate on occasion. I wonder if there is an atheist in a successful loving relationship who does not live by these words of Jesus. I wonder if there is any who treats their wife or husband like they hate to be treated (the opposite ethic from that of Jesus) and has a successful and good relationship. I think we all can answer that.

- We are left with reason and logic, and how the application of these rules for sound thinking to these opposite beliefs either confirm them or question their viability and validity. Use sound rationality and logic, and don't follow the foolish idea that reason and logic are not valid tools for finding truth — and by the way, also for finding a rewarding life. Yes, postmodernism wants you to forsake logic and reason and believe in what is left (the opposite of logic and reason): your own opinion, whether it makes sense of not.

- Everyone has, either consciously or unconsciously, a sense about the origin of this universe. Everyone can evaluate the evidence about God's handiwork and what it is consistently telling us about his reality. The right faith will make all the difference to the quality of our lives if we seek to live consistently by its tenets.

- This belief, as we will see, whichever one you adopt, will determine the direction for everything you think and everything you do — everything about God, this universe, and ourselves. What we think and believe is us. "As a man thinks … so is he."

Which faith is yours? Start your journey evaluating the evidence provided in *Compelling Evidence for God*, and then face the reality of what your belief will do for you and how you will affect the lives of others, too. Don't forget, we don't live to ourselves. We cannot.

Beliefs Lead to Actions

We all act, eventually, according to our beliefs. That's why it is so important to sort out our beliefs. Our beliefs unconsciously influence our actions, whether we are thinking about them or not. Therefore, our lives are sometimes determined by unwise or false beliefs. We may change a belief in the last split second before we act, or keep oscillating back and forth. But we still act on our beliefs in the end.

The Story of a Word

Words have histories, and we will pause to remind ourselves of the interesting history of the word *morals*. It's a word that invades more of our decisions than we may be ready to admit.

We begin in Greece. Social life needed some form of structure. Every society that has formed its culture has usually included rules of conduct, written or expected in its culture's structure. The Greeks called these rules *nomoi*. Rules soon became laws, but many unwritten and unlegalized rules of conduct became customs, and they, in turn, soon became what was expected of all people. The Greeks coined the word *ethos* for these customary rules of conduct. So, *ethos* took on the meaning of what was normal, expected, mannerly, and customary.

Enter Cicero (106-43 BC), a Roman. Taking the Greek word *ethos* or *ethikos*, he formed the Latin word *moralis* from it, and from that word, we get our word "morals." The Greek meaning of *ethos* carried over into both the Latin and English words and also came to be seen as normal expected behavior, mannerly, and customary.

Cicero was a highly educated man and, being very ambitious, he entered politics. However, he had a lot of trouble with the word he formed: *moralis*. Flaunting what was customary, he was unwise in this choice of winners in politics. And because he was also unmannerly and did not keep to the norms expected of a person in his position, it was only with luck he survived an attempt on his life. He was subsequently, for similar behavior, exiled under Clodius, was recalled, and lost his political integrity when he tried to play both opposing sides in politics (unmannerly behavior and not the expected norm), which caught up with him again. Once more, making a wrong choice of winners, he delivered a famous speech against Anthony, who then set sights on eliminating him. Anthony's soldiers caught him as he attempted to escape and murdered him. His lack of morals (what was normal behavior, expected, and mannerly) was his downfall. Indeed fortunate, he lived to 63. You might say he was remembered for his behavior as a slippery snake, and snakes lack morals.

People have always had trouble with their morals. Morals are not in vogue today either, but for some, they play a part in their choice of God or no God. Here's a typical example of how making a decision over morals can affect our belief in the existence of God or no God.

When faced with making a moral decision...

1. The one who does not believe in God may make their moral decisions with an air of "anything can be both right and wrong; it all depends on your perception of things." They think any absolute rules for morals don't apply to them. They feel they can best form their own moral beliefs, and even think they have a right to do so because it is their life. Usually, for them, moral issues are decided on the principle of what is most convenient or beneficial in the moment. By excluding God, they naturally become the center of their own universe.

2. The one who believes in God is usually more poignantly aware of the reality of right and wrong, as seen in the nature that is described in the Bible of God. The standard for all actions is what God has said is the best way to live, because he does what is right, what is righteous. They should also become aware of how other people should be treated with dignity and respect. Why? Because their actions should be founded on their belief that all people are made in the image of God. Creatures of God should behave with love, seek truth, and act like their creator. This person finds that everything in their life is conditioned by what God's will for them is, and they believe this is their path to real happiness. These people follow a higher authority.

Inability to decide what to believe is no escape from the consequences of our beliefs and actions, especially those moral actions. When we believe that there are no universal laws that apply to everyone, we are acting like the dimwitted ostrich that hides its head in the sand in the hopes it will escape what it does not want to face.

What makes the postmodernist philosophy so lame is that it ignores the realities of life itself. We cannot escape the logic and effects of natural consequences on our lives, or the law of cause and effect, or the absolute reality of the law of gravity. We are, in fact, in charge of our own lives. Our decisions shape our lives. Consequences imply a right and a wrong because they convey a warning or a congratulations for our decisions. All our decisions are choices between consequences. Consequences are inevitable. Therefore, we can't avoid right and wrong, good and bad, truth and its ugly opposite, or reality itself.

Making the Main Decision

So, if intelligence, purpose, and design are written everywhere, overwhelmingly, in the universe and as a result, we only have two choices to help us answer the question of how did the universe originate, here are the choices...

Alternative One:
The source of this universe must be an intelligent source. The source would have to have the capacity to think, plan, and create an intelligent universe. Intelligence also necessitates that the source must be a living entity (have life). Alternative

one is that life preexisted the universe in a non-material form. This life brought into being all things material and formed humans of material and non-material elements. Humans were made in the image of this preexistent life (God). This is the message of Genesis, Chapter One: "In the beginning, God [who preexisted creation]… created the heavens and the earth… and made humans in his own image." Rehearsing what we know of ourselves, we can begin to flesh out the fuller meaning of the words "in his image": personhood, etc. We are told where to look to find evidence for this alternative: the heavens and the earth and all that is in them. This evidence proves to be overwhelmingly in favor of this alternative. Science progresses daily, amazingly, with discovering the facts in our universe. These facts and others, not speculations, form the solid evidence that we can depend upon.

Alternative Two:

Intelligence, purpose, and design, which we find in the design of living creatures had to come from somewhere. That somewhere, or something, if not intelligent (as alternative one maintains), was an unintelligent source with no mind or capacity to think, plan, or create. A biological theory of evolution has to begin with unintelligent, lifeless substances, which in a process described as natural selection form the story of our origins. However, this story never actually addresses the question of origins, but accepts the answers (speculations) that are given by other scientific disciplines about the beginning of this universe. Because it does not advocate or require a Creator-God for its theories, or any reality other than matter in some form or other, it has been the "go to" alternative for all who do not want to think of an intelligent living source, like God, as the creator of the universe. However, this alternative raises several issues that are very real problems. Here are some of these difficulties that this alternative will have to convincingly surmount.

- Everything would have developed from an unintelligent source. We are told it did so by tiny incremental changes, as in Darwin's biological theory. In the final analysis, natural selection (the method for these incremental changes) would likewise be an unintelligent process. If however, as the words natural selection suggest, we are asked to believe or infer that natural selection knew what was needed for survival, it would posses some sort of primitive intelligence. If it was not natural selection that was in some way intelligent, the intelligence would have to be assigned to some other force at work in nature that created the same hypothetical results. The problem arises when we are forced to ask, "Where did the jump from unintelligent matter to primitive intelligent urges, at best, come from?"

- We would have to be told of an adequate cause for intelligence to rise out of unintelligence, not just be given a supposed explanation of how it happened (which is not supplied, and if it was, it would be theory, not fact). All explanations, if indeed factually correct, are only descriptions of how something happens. They fall far short of finding the *cause* of what happened. Evidence that is compelling is needed to help us determine what this cause was — whether intelligent or not. We have compelling evidence for the intelligent design of a human, for example. The most likely cause of this intelligent design is an intelligent designer, which this alternative denies.

- Those tiny incremental changes, which we are told happened over billions of years in the process of natural selection, are in themselves nothing but a semantic, theoretical attempt to make natural selection more believable. If you are faced with what appears to be an impossible leap (such as from unintelligence to intelligence), then you are left with few options. The theory of natural selection, then, must help people make that leap by adding two options: that it took billions of years, and that the leap was made in tiny increments. But that doesn't solve the problem. The leap from unintelligence to intelligence has simply been avoided (circumvented) by way of trying to make it more believable. All we are given is a theory with no evidence to support the billions of years or the need for tiny increments. It compounds the problem while not solving it. The fact remains: intelligence and life cannot arise out of unintelligent substances. The choice of the words "natural selection" was a clever way of trying to get around it all looking like chance happenings. The jump from unintelligence to intelligence remains insurmountable. Again we ask, where is the proof that life can be born out of lifeless, inanimate matter? Where is the proof or evidence for any of this desperate theory?

• The theory of evolution is a biological answer to how living creatures developed. It is increasingly being used as an explanation for almost everything. Why should we be told to believe that our emotions have evolved without any evidence to support the speculation? Without evidence and with only a theory to substantiate the claim, this is also obviously, crooked thinking.

So, there it is — the big decision, the one we have to settle first: Which alternative treats the evidence of intelligent design more honestly? We have two very different understandings of how the world came into existence and has come to be what it is today. Only one of the two alternatives is reasonable. Only one makes any sense at all.

Which Alternative Is the Best?

Which is the most reasonable and rational belief that will give meaning to our lives and an explanation of an adequate source for our universe? Is it the leap of faith to an intelligent source, or the leap of faith to a lifeless evolution of natural forces that possess no intelligence? We cannot live happily with a philosophy that means life comes from an unintelligent and meaningless source. If our source possessed no intelligence, neither could we!

It certainly appears from the evidence we saw in *Compelling Evidence for God* that God is the more intelligent and reasonable answer. If, however, you choose the unintelligent source as the correct answer, the questions that are left unanswered — plus the stubborn fact that everything we know and have known about life and our world is evidence against this alternative — leave us with what seems like an unintelligent choice. The answers from those who cannot bear the thought of an intelligent source feel like they have to exclude an intelligent source for the universe. Again, they turn out to be nothing but unproven suppositions or crooked arguments with no solid evidence to back them up. This makes it even more intelligently acceptable and necessary to believe in the first alternative: an intelligent source, backed with tangible and overwhelming evidence.

Let's put what we have argued in the form of what may be a helpful checklist. This way, the complicated issue is broken down into bitesized pieces. Each decision boils down to alternative one or two.

- How can intelligent life emerge unaided from material elements that have no life or intelligence without intelligent help? Put another way, how can an inert substance have the knowledge or capability to produce itself as a living substance? Place a rock into a scientific lab and, even if you keep it there for billions of years, ask yourself, "Is it likely to produce life?" Lifeless matter is a non-starter. It is an idea that hasn't seen the light of day. To put our faith in this leap and call it the most intelligent leap is, well, you know: far-fetched. So, decide. Alternative one or two? Which?

- How can lifeless matter be individually "programed" so as to become the necessary software for each form of life we see in the universe? (We will answer these first two questions in greater detail in the chapter "I Am a Living Creature". Hold these two until you have read Chapter Four.)

- An intelligent and purposefully functioning design requires a designer. Or it doesn't? Does a purposefully functioning design just happen without a designer? Don't think of just one. Think of countless purposeful designs, all acting to create a functional human system. Think of the impossibility of chance making all this happen so that the human form could live and function properly. Ask this, "Can splashing paint on a wall produce a Mona Lisa?" You should know the answer to that one. Splashing the paint and producing such a detailed and wonderful piece of art would actually be a less complicated task than designing all the functioning cells of the human body and having them all successfully support, sustain, and give life and intelligence to it. Your choice then: alternative one or two?

- Where could intelligent life most likely have come from? Alternative one or two? Don't fear what others might think of you for your answer. Have you noticed that if your answer is alliterative one, you will be treated as if there must be something wrong with the question — or more likely, with you, the questioner. Have you also noticed, children will make you feel there is something wrong with you when they don't like your answer?

- If the universe showed convincing signs of intelligence at its very first nanosecond of existence, how can we avoid the conclusion that intelligence was behind the initial activity? Alternative one or two? (See *Compelling Evidence for God*, page 25 ff, for the details to this question).

- Finally, you may have noticed the absence of any reference to the world of the immaterial and its spiritual realities. There is even denial of the reality of anything non-material by those who choose alternative two. This is a question that begs to be answered. Is the world only matter? Or is it matter and spirit? It's hard to find a word for something like spirit because it refers to something intangible. Hard, because words themselves are tangible things. But we have to make an attempt. So in the meantime, let's use the word spirit. Theories about what the human spirit is — when we can obviously sense and experience things like self-consciousness, mind, soul and spiritual realities in ourselves — are, as you might imagine, many. The reason it is hard for some to come to terms with these human realities is because they are not matter that can be examined, felt, and sensed. Therefore, for those who believe there is nothing that is not of a material nature in our universe or in us humans, they simply scoff at the mention of a human spirit. That's the cunning of sophistry. To them, our sense of these things are the elephant in the room that atheists refuse to acknowledge. Neither is it a forgone or reasonable conclusion, as some insist, that the human spirit must be a form of matter somehow. The philosophy that undergirds much of science, which says there isn't anything but matter in the universe, dies a very hard death.

If you choose the second alternative, think also of the following. You have chosen what must be an amazing creator and designer who deserves a divine title. Is that designer chance? Is it able to accomplish what we can only imagine an all-powerful and intelligent God could create? The universe and all its creatures, including we humans, are a mind boggling achievement. And that is what makes sense for those with open minds to believe in alternative one. So why the hesitancy to accept God as the source? Is it because you can't imagine a being so great, who could think up and create such an amazing universe? If you are choosing the second alternative, could it be that your faith in this alternative as a viable alternative to an intelligent source is not fully comprehending the amazing evidence of design, purpose, and intelligence in our universe.

Further, what does alternative two tell us about the value of the world we live in and our value as creatures if we believe we have been formed without the need of any intelligence in an evolutionary process that was driven by chance? Who, then, are you? If we have evolved by chance, then chance is by far the greatest law in the universe, dwarfing the mysteries of all laws, even the law of gravity (which incidentally, chance would have been responsible for, too). Design by chance is, by the way, an oxymoron. It is an oversight for humans to not have created an international shrine in its honor, if it is the cause of all.

Chance is not the god that you would want in charge at the helm of all things in the universe, especially if you are about to be wheeled in for surgery. You would much rather, I'm sure, seek confidence in your intelligent design and its inbuilt laws of healing and recovery, and that your surgeon is intelligent and reliably designed, too.

A world that comes from unintelligence has no meaning either. How can it? So ask, "Can we honestly live as though we and our wife/husband and kids have no meaning to us — no meaning at all, just an accident?" Your child could kill you and it would have no meaning. Your spouse could treat your marriage as though it had no meaning and not take any responsibility for such actions, into the bargain. Whenever life gets rough, you could find the only sensible answer in taking your own life because, after all, it too has no meaning. Your teen might tell you their cell phone has no meaning. That would be the only up side. You may not have thought about that. But no teen will tell you that, anyhow!

Of course, we can't live happily that way. Life and all of its rich emotions would have no meaning; nor would work or play, love or hate, even life or death. We would have to agree we are a hapless, tragic accident. Life's hard times cannot be endured when the truth is that unintelligent hapless happenings are all there is to who we are. Choose the alternative that gives you the greatest meaning in life.

You might be thinking your achievements have meaning, though? They do to you, at times, and perhaps also to others. However, **it's not what you have achieved, but who you are by nature** that is the real you. Who you are is where real meaning lives. This is all about finding true meaning in who you are: a creature made in the image of God and loved by God. Ask the down-and-outs, the homeless, and they will tell you, meaning is in being loved, which is the same as saying being valued. We will never have to face that sickening feeling of worthlessness when we know we *are* someone and *are loved* by someone. Could I say, at least by the person who brought us into being in the first place?

Which is the greater leap of faith: accepting that unintelligent matter magically produced intelligence and life, or accepting that intelligence of the scope found in the design of the universe came from the actions and will of an intelligent being? Any real objection to giving that being a name: God?

Takeaway Points

- Always keep the evidence from intelligent design in mind. The source of our amazing world should be seen in how it is made: there has to be a designer behind an intelligent design.

- Our beliefs shape our lives. We must never forget this. Decide your beliefs carefully.

- We all have a vague belief about where our world came from. However vague and hazy it may be, however right or wrong, it will set the course for all else in our lives.

- Chose between the two alternatives, and that will begin to settle the biggest question of all for you. You don't have to be a brilliant mind to do this (although, with a mind made in the image of God, you are more brilliant that you think you are — provided, of course, you use it). You have used it to read this far, so congratulations! Start thinking big about yourself.

- It's not just the evidence of intelligent design we find in the universe that should lead to your decision, but the use of reason and logic as well. You and I must have a faith that is of the head as well as the heart.

- To believe in an unintelligent source for the world will bring to you no sense of intrinsic worth. But you know you have intrinsic worth, don't you? Your consciousness of who and what you are tells you that.

- We can't live without feeling worthy, and our beliefs are where that sense of worthiness comes from. Our beliefs must find a sufficient reason for who we are and give a real sense of worth to us, or life is not worth living.

- The more we think about it, the more the choice of chance being our "god" appears very mindless. We are intelligent, believe it or not. That leaves us no other alternative but the first. Let's form our beliefs about who we are and how we should live.

Teaching Tools

Teach the above takeaway points.

• Help your children understand and appreciate how nature and all that we know about our world show that it is designed. Use the flowers, trees, how our bodies show design (such as in our blood system, our eyes, our hands). Impress them with these designs and how they could not have come about by chance. Keep teaching the design that is all around us and do this as you, too, discover more of the design in our world. A convenient treatment of obvious evidence for design can be found in *How We May Know that God Is — Simple Evidence About God for Young People* by William W. Orr.

• Find songs for children that speak of God's creation.

• Find praise songs that exalt the creative acts of God. There are many.

• Make the point over and over again that a design doesn't just happen; it needs a designer. Make that point in all the actions of daily life: our clothes, food, play, etc.

• For girls who are into clothing fashions in particular, visit a designer clothing store and talk about the designs and their designer. Careful! You may part with some of your hard-earned cash.

• View paintings and artwork and talk of how art must have an artist. Talk about God as the great artist of the universe.

- Comment constantly that every intelligently designed thing has a purpose and learn more of the purpose behind the human designs of aircraft, etc. Ask and comment about how an aircraft, or car, or any amazing human creation must have had a designer, and if so, how the universe and all that is in it must also have had a designer.

- Talk about how designs are made.

- Keep showing them how intelligent God was in how he made everything in nature to work. Our bodies are full of evidence of how things grow and work for a purpose.

- Design does not have to function perfectly to be a design. A design, for a human, must first be functional and beautiful. But it is a design that we can cause to malfunction.

4 — I Am a Valuable Living Creature

Well, I hope you are enjoying your life.

It is going to be very informative and interesting to ask yourself "Where did the life I am enjoying come from? What is life? What kind of a creature am I? Does my life have any worth? Can we make life in a lab or clone it, somehow?"

There are multitudes of questions about life to which science has no answers, just speculations at best. And that's no put-down of science, because life is a very real puzzle. We need more than science to tell us all we need to know about life.

To create life requires a living being who has life to pass it on and understands how to make something live — some living being with the intelligence to design a creature that can meaningfully experience life with all its wonders. Of course, not a something or an inanimate substance, not even a nonliving process that has no consciousness. We will uncover the impossibility of this last sentence and the sense of the previous sentence as we proceed.

Life and Computers

Biologists love to compare life to a computer. This is how. Just like a computer, life must first build its hardware. Our hardware is a string of molecules (chemicals), all linked together to form our DNA. Then we need the information, which is encoded and embedded in the DNA and all our cells, for life to begin to be a meaningful possibility. This encoded information is our software. A computer with hardware and no software is, well, useless. Now, ask any middle school student, "How is software made?" He/she will tell you, "By a person who writes code and designs software programs."

The biologists are using the analogy of a computer to help people understand what life is like. The analogy is used to back off from the details and enable the overall picture to be more clearly understood in terms non-biologists can understand. Analogies are like parables. They are not to be pressed for an explanation of their every detail. Rather, they make one point clear to all who hear them. This is what the author of a parable wants to achieve.

To summarize, scientists use analogies in a similar fashion:

• First, to simplify so that we don't get lost in the details.

• Second, to clarify what the details are telling us so that, without a trained knowledge of the science involved in the details, the average person can comprehend quickly and accurately the main point.

• Third, analogies are also used to give us a bird's eye view so that we see the relationships of the details to the whole and understand the overall purpose and function of the whole — the end result that the details serve.

With this in mind, we will take what the biologists have done and understand where that analogy might lead us. In the process, we will learn more about the origin of humans, the mystery of life, the complexity of the human system, and the only answer that can sensibly account for the appearance of the human creature. Our inestimable value will become clear.

Who we are will be realistically seen, and all that will be left for us will be to believe in ourselves and accept who the "real me" is.

Our Hardware

Scientists have been hard at work to create a DNA chain of molecules that would house life. We will think of our DNA and the cellular structure of the body as our hardware. Chemicals are part of the matter that makes up the material universe and, of course, this includes our DNA. Scientists are very good at working with chemicals — any material substance, for that matter.

They have been working on the hardware for quite a long time. As yet, we have no complete identification and arrangement of molecules in the lab that would form the hardware. The first requirement for life is its hardware. In the case of humans, it means a living, working hardware, not anything as simple as the hardware we build for a computer.

There is still a long way for our scientists to go, because they must somehow create life, which is the real heart of the problem. There is no life without an adequate living hardware, so this is where to start. They may arrange existing living molecules, but that is not the same as creating life or its hardware from inanimate substances in the first place, of course. Their efforts are, however, highlighting the mystery, value, and difficulty of creating a living human being.

Our Software

Something else beside hardware is needed. The middle schooler told us: the writing of code and the creating of software.

If you want to create this living human being, we will need to have information written in special code (code is, of course, the computer's language with which it communicates) — a code that will meet the needs and the requirements of human software. We will have to embed this living software as operating instructions for a living organism into the living hardware. Do you think that's gong to be simple?

That word *living* is going to pose multiple challenges and create demands the designer and creator of a computer does not have to face. So the analogy will break down at that point. However, let's continue to use the analogy for further elucidation.

This software is the really tricky part of the process for evolution and the evolutionary methodology of natural selection to accomplish, since it is information that is needed, not the creation and use of physical substances like was needed for the hardware. These operating instructions for each cell of the body are transmitted by chemical and electromagnetic communication systems throughout the body. The information (code) uses these systems, plus others, to communicate its messages.

That it must begin as operating instructions, written for the human system by some form of intelligence (what the middle schooler told us was done by a person) now comes into play. This is the part that is so often not elucidated. In simple words, it is software (which the designer of the computer has first imagined, then translated what is imagined into code so the imagined design can become working software) that is needed. The imagined design (at this stage, non-material in nature) is in a special form of information or operating instructions only for functioning in human cells. This information, for the sake of simplicity, is then translated into substances that the human body can use for whatever purpose the information dictates. The imagination and writing of code and its translation (into a working physical system to make it functional) requires intelligence of a very high order. Leaving this to chance or natural selection to imagine raises what are insurmountable obstacles.

Natural selection, the method evolution is said to have used, is supposed to be able to identify the next piece of matter that is needed so that the physical evolving of the human can continue. But natural selection has no ability to create, imagine, and design. Information is not, before it is written, of a physical nature, even though it may use physical means of communication after it has been installed.

Here are the simple logical requirements for a well designed piece of software and for our human software, as well. First, it has to be thought of and imagined. Then, the instructions must be set in a form the hardware can read (the code). And then, the hardware must have the ability to read it. It is still missing one very important piece. It is with this requirement that the analogy again fails. The software must meet all the requirements of a *living changing and growing* organism that has an extremely intelligent mental system headquartered in the mind/brain. Constant new operational instructions will need to be written to meet the demands of the software's multiple apps and the changing environmental challenges the system faces. Just thinking, alone, will require a lot of imagination and instructions.

We don't know all the information that is required for the complex human system to fully and in a coordinated fashion operate, nor how to encode it into a living substance. If we, with all of our intelligence, don't know how, what, where, and when to do all this, how did natural selection, which has no mind, figure all this out?

Complicate this further with the need for each cell to have information peculiar to that cell encoded in it somehow — while not being encoded in the wrong cell, of course. For example, we don't want to end up with the cells that form the ear being encoded and implanted by mistake in the nose, producing a nose that looks like an ear. That would be embarrassing, even for natural selection!

At this point let's ask, can natural selection, the principle that is crucial to the theory of evolution, actually make all of these "tiny steps over billions of years" happen (and as Richard Dawkins informs us, these are the requirements for Natural Selection to be successful) and succeed, when many of these tiny steps must happen simultaneously or the whole living project dies.

Let's revisit the timing factor. Both the physical and nonphysical steps must be happening on time and, unfortunately for the human system, thousands of them will be needed at the same time because the human system is "infinitely" complex. If delivery is not on time, this living human system will not function for lack of an essential element that was late or not yet ready. In a living system, disaster will certainly strike. Natural selection is clearly an inadequate principle to achieve all this, especially the elements that are not physical but are the intelligent operating instructions imagined and designed for the project in the first place.

Don't let this pass you by: the human system, with all its functions and unbelievable detail seen in the biological studies of the human cells, is extremely complex. It can't be broken down into tiny steps over billions of years (or even for a day, in many cases) because it is clearly, to any knowledgeable student, irreducibly complex. Can't do it little by little without this living system dying as it waits for delivery of parts that should have arrived seconds ago, let alone millions of years ago.

The principle of Natural Selection has no intelligence, mind, purpose, goal, or plan in mind. (Oops! It has no mind or, for that matter, any way of guiding its steps). It functions by responding to immediate needs only — again, without a plan, purpose, design, or goal to guide it. Why would we even begin to think of it as an adequate theory of how a human came to be?

Requirements To Make Human Software

The following are some of the requirements and specifications peculiar to our human software:

The Nature of Human Software

- Software is encoded information. Information is not physical matter that scientists can manipulate or elements of some sort that nature could select. "Select" is the wrong word, of course. To "select" suggests intelligent action, which Darwin was trying to avoid. The choice of intelligence (as the answer to how we came to be) belonged to Paley. Our software, being nonmaterial in nature, is better described in a concept as "informational operating procedures." That's something evolution or natural selection has no ability to understand, let alone deal with. Therefore, natural selection, when attempting this kind of task, is a blind warrior in a sword fight.

- The middle schooler got something else right. He would tell you that a computer's software is written by a person. For human software, we might say, "…by an intelligent being who has the qualities of a person and, perhaps, more." Apparently, Darwin didn't think of this when he tried to better Paley's argument that a design required a designer. His answer was that no designer was needed; natural selection will do all that is necessary to produce life, thank you.

- Because of the irreducible complexity and the needed functionality of the human design, it had to have been a very clever designer who wrote the extremely detailed software information without anything being left out. Failure to think of all the requirements for a living organism would be fatal to the project. A functional, complex design could not be waiting for a piece to be added to make it work. It would immediately malfunction. The digestive system is a functional design and is irreducibly complex. If it were still in the process of being built and some section or task of the digestive tract was not functional yet or still in the process of being built, the human would soon die a painful death. Of course, this requirement eliminates a long process of evolution by blind natural selection.

- The software from some other animal would not be adequate for installation in a human. Natural selection would have to be aware of the different needs and not short change the needs of the more advanced creature.

- Different cells have different functions. The software would have to be written specifically for the purpose and functioning of the cell. This baffles our minds. Was it of no consequence to Darwin and his followers? It seems obvious to the unprofessional observer that different parts of the body function in different ways and may have different needs. Paley drew attention to this, even without the knowledge we have today that is far more sophisticated.

- The designer of this software would have to be a living person who understood the needs of a living person's software. The only thing that makes sense is that a real person designed and created the living person. Who could that be?

- The needs and the requirements and goals of any construction have to be understood at the beginning of a project. Otherwise, if building a house or creating a creature, the desired result will be haphazard and may, without guidance each step of the way, fail. And the best will not be achieved. A human is such an amazing creation, it is unthinkable that there was no plan followed from the beginning. It's time to say, if a theory doesn't make any sense because it contradicts what we humans know of our human reality, try some other theory. Natural selection is a very inadequate theory to explain who we are or to qualify for being the creator, or even the director, of human software.

- The process of evolution by natural selection is devoid of intelligence. If evolutionists are going to claim natural selection has a form of primitive intelligence, they are claiming it is an intelligent process. That is exactly what Paley argued: a design necessitates an intelligent designer. Darwin denied that to be true and thought he had a better answer. By the way, that knowledge would have to be greater than what humans posses, because if we judge by our present state of knowledge, we could not do it. Can we reasonably believe that natural selection has a greater intelligence than humans have demonstrated? It must have achieved its amazing results in blind fashion, achieving something we cannot do, even with our eyes wide open to the biochemistry of the human cellular structure and its design. That's elevating a blind process to a status that defies logic and sense. Not to mention, our scientists should be offended!

- Can this non-living principle of natural selection, when faced with a fork in its evolutionary road, take the right fork? Yes. Can it take the wrong fork? Yes. Can it take the right fork at the wrong time? Yes. Can it take the wrong fork at the right time? Yes. Can it skip making a decision and hope for the best? Yes. It takes its steps without a mind to think or intelligence to guide it. What can we expect from this process of mindless selection? Anything! That is, anything can happen. What's another name for "anything can happen"? Chance.

- It is relevant to note: One of our software languages (there are several communication languages in our physical system) is electromagnetic currents. There are many variations in these currents, conveying different messages. They are not completely readable to us, but we can recognize they are an intelligent way to send non-material messages through a material system. How could natural selection have designed and fashioned this phenomenon without amazing intelligence? There is no use in denying that it shows all the evidence of design. A language, whether it be in written form or in the form of chemical elements, is still a design. It is the arrangements of ideas and elements to achieve a given purpose: namely, the transporting of a message in order to activate a system to function and achieve the goal the message intended. We cannot think straight of natural selection without factoring in the foregone undeniable conclusion that the human is designed. So you see, the situation is building up to be more than chance (or natural selection) is equipped to handle. We can't avoid the logic of Paley's argument that the purposeful design found in a human being certainly requires nothing less than a designer!

- This operational code has to be written to meet all the demands of a living human. Not just any code will do that. It has to be a code for both giving, sustaining, and managing life in a living system as it operates in circumstances unknown to it and, often times, surprising it. All natural selection apparently did was to observe that some tiny change was for the betterment of the species and, therefore, for its apparent survival. Fat chance, that such an improbability will result in the most complex and astounding design we have ever seen: the total human system. Natural selection, by nature, is an uncertain decision that may be right or may turn out to be a hindrance to the rest of the functioning living system. Who knows? It is not driven by knowledge and the intelligent use of knowledge. This is not a story that leads to the creation of a fantastic design, but to a fluky move — a constant game of hit-or-miss.

- The information required to operate the human system is actually much more than a simple code. To meet the software's requirements, it must operate and manage...
  - The trillion or more cells in the human body:
  - The supply of nutrition to all of them,
  - Disposal of waste from the energy required for our cells' constant operations,

- Keeping a finely tuned heating/cooling system functioning with precision,
- Controlling the surges of intelligent emotions and coordinating with the entire mental system to manage the ill results of unintelligent emotions, along with the stress they cause,
- Directing and managing an army of cells to attack all invaders, including viruses,
- Repairing damaged cells,
- Birthing new cells,
- Reproducing other humans in a way absolutely unique to the needs of a human,
- Interacting, all the while, with the needs of our changing environment,
- And much, much more — all from a central station.

That station, being a mental system of brain and mind, must remain actively monitoring everything, 24/7 for a lifetime, "…through sickness and health, for better or for worse, until death do us part," and keep a healthy balance between all the systems in the process. In other words, this is undeniably a designed operation, meeting numerous needs. Sorry, but unintelligent principles, forces, or happenings are a certain non-starter.

- This communication system would have to be far more advanced than all of our most intelligent technologies put together. Please ponder the human system's obvious design while thinking of the implications of its irreducible complexity and the vastness of its scale. Ask yourself how this can come to be. Some people (who would feel insulted if they were not addressed as intelligent) think this came about by a blind process that lacked intelligence, dubbed "natural selection." Something does not ring true about that conclusion. It is plainly inadequate and would not be

chosen as the best candidate for human development —
especially by intelligent humans.

Ingenious Plus

Our software's informational code, as we have pointed out, is
ingeniously written. Its author should be a shoe-in for a Nobel
Prize. It is ingenious, if ingenious is knowledge far beyond our
human comprehension. If indeed you still think natural
selection is the best and only viable explanation of how we
have come to be what we are, keep trying to convince us.
You'll have to do better than an evolutionary process of
natural selection. We instinctively know we are much more
than what an unintelligent source could produce. Words fail
us to describe the wonder of who we are, but perhaps this is
a good attempt: "We are fearfully and wonderfully made," the
words of the psalmist. If you are looking for a good choice for
the intelligent designer of us, God will end up being the only
one on the list.

A Few More Facts for the Unconvinced to Ponder

- We also know that cells can be coopted to perform tasks
  that are not native to their programing. They can learn and
  reprogram themselves, apparently, to aid the work of other
  cells. Our system has been designed to foresee such a
  need and responds quickly to an overload with whatever
  reprograming is needed. When such a need arises, it does
  not have to wait for natural selection's snail-pace process
  to fashion a change to meet a sudden need. Natural
  selection is incapable of this "in-the-moment, split-second
  reprograming." Multiple changes at high speed is only
  achieved by an outstanding design. Think of the split
  second communications and sudden changes seen in, let's

say, a military jet. We never doubt that it has been designed by an intelligent process.

- Another step natural selection couldn't have engineered is the various required speeds we find operative in a human system. Speeds from the comparative tortoise pace of thinking to the hare's speed of emotional arousal. It has to program the reception of information from one cell and forward it to, perhaps, millions of affected cells, while updating that information virtually instantaneously. There is obvious purpose in our design everywhere we look. Stub your toe and how long do you have to wait before you know it? We experience it instantly. The brain, for example, is changing every moment, too, at the speed of thought. When we think, feel, and decide, appropriate changes happen to the brain's landscape at astounding speeds. In the flash of a moment, literally billions of cells are in action and within those cells, countless chemical elements are being manufactured, transported, and are preforming their needed tasks while we go about the actions of fulfilling the demands of daily living. Are you getting an idea of how significant you must be in the world of living things to be designed with such precision and care?

- We know even less about the mind than we do about the brain. We are aware of the results the mind produces, but little knowledge of the intricate operation of its transmissions. If we only knew it all, we would be awestruck. The more we know about ourselves, the faster the impending funeral for the theory of natural selection approaches. It will, however, be attended by all who are still passionate to eliminate the idea of God.

Growth and Maintenance Issues

- The encoded information we are talking about (the human software) has the ability to provide each cell with the instructions to grow and develop without a pause, while the human system continues to perform at full speed — no shut downs. What would have happened if this complex system were put together one-tiny-step-after-another over billions of years? It is a theory that reason, perhaps, all too quietly scoffs at. It is an irreducible design that will cease to exist at any stage of its development if all of its essential parts and functions are not in place to operate as designed. It can't function and do all we need it to do if it is not a complete system. So imagine what happened in the evolutionary calendar when everything had to wait for the body's waste disposal system to be finished and the waste satisfactorily dispelled, or the sensitive heating system to be up and running. This makes the billions of years evolution required to put all these pieces together (one mini step after another) strongly suggest it could never have happened that way.

- An intelligent designer would not have put up with this kind of incompetence. Restarts would have to occur at every incomplete or wrong step that natural selection allowed to happen. Irreducible complexity is an impossible mountain for undesigned progress to climb. One can see clearly, without any knowledge of the chemistry of biology, that it can't be built one-molecule-after-another, waiting for available elements to show up or making some wrong step without causing its own demise. The human design certainly could not have watched for updates and then shut down for a while to allow for new information to be downloaded and installed, like a computer must. This is life we are talking about, which can't be told to wait for essentials.

- There is undeniable evidence that from the moment of conception, the human DNA is designed with all it needs to grow and develop according to plan. We can actually forecast what human DNA will develop into: a human — not an ape or a wolf. We could not do that if the "design" were not written all over it and in the DNA — and also the structure of our body and mind and stamped in its growth process from the very beginning. Know the DNA, and we know the end result. Know a seed's DNA, and we know what plant or kind of tree it will produce. It is the element we recognize as design that makes this kind of process so reliably predictable.

- A design does not necessitate that the end result has to be perfect either, or operate perfectly under all conditions. Human abuses of the human body and even our environment can result in a malfunction and an imperfect result. Humans will admit to such abuse.

Individual Design

And here is yet another clincher. This software has to be designed for each individual human — not just for humans in general — or for the differences in the function of the cells. Why? Because all of us are unique, with different bodies, temperaments, and strengths that serve different purposes with different skill levels. Cells that express themselves one way form one individual and express themselves another way to form a different individual. DNA (hardware) has its own secrets of how it can be expressed differently, meaning much of our DNA does not mean only one result can happen.

- And how is this going to be engineered? Temperament supplies an example. The basic urges and drives that are inherent in an individual and that shape that person's life, are quite different in each individual. Each person is engineered differently. How did natural selection create an infinite variety so that we are unique with no known clone somewhere else among the billions of human beings? Temperament's characteristics are in us at birth. They are not the result of our different environmental factors. We do show adaptations, however — one being when we adopt strengths from other temperaments that are due, perhaps, to the influences of our upbringing, or environmental pressures, or the demands of our job that produce the need. The basic urges and drives do not change. We also know these basic urges and drives form their unique expressions in each of the temperaments, as any frustrated parent can bear witness to.

- Temperament is not a physical entity, either. It is not passed on by heredity, as is clearly seen in identical twins who do not have identical temperaments. Ask the parents. Children often turn out to have temperaments different from their parents, too, which causes some parents not to understand their children.

- These temperaments also appear in distinct and recognizable patterns. The same recognizable patterns are evident in different races and in different countries, which have different lifestyles and cultures. Is all this, too, a result of natural selection, chance happenings?

- Wow! This diversity is asking more than any of us expected of the source of our software. And yet, someone is trying to get us to believe it all happened without purpose or design. That's attributing to natural selection a plan, which it does not have, and on a scale it does not even recognize. Thinking that it happened without any intelligent purpose or design is asking too much of an unintelligent source.

No Hardware in the Lab Yet?

Yet we are so much smarter and intelligent than this thoughtless process. So let's pause and note: the hardware has to first be fashioned to be the receptor for all the encoded information — the software. Our scientists are lagging far behind what some believe natural selection already accomplished at least thousands of years ago. Add to this the fact that we are starting with billions of humans (the finished product) to observe and study (an advantage natural selection didn't have, and if it did, it could not comprehend the significance of the concept of advantage). Remember, natural selection has no mind to think and plan. We already know the goal and purpose we want to achieve in the lab, and we are intelligent, so why is it we still don't understand life fully?

• Admittedly, natural selection had, according to its advocates, billions of years to produce us. But it started with no goal or purpose in mind (it has no mental faculties), no intelligence, and no life to pass on. Imagine a rock after lying in a lab for billions of years. It would still be a rock, having made no progress in coming alive, true? So the first hurdle for evolution and materialism to surmount is the creation of life.

• We have understood that the encoded messages in our software are information — not chemical in nature, even though chemicals are involved in the conveyance of the information. They are the second impossibility for natural selection to solve. These messages use material elements for the transmission of the message (chemical and electromagnetic systems) in the brain and elsewhere in the body. But the hardware (the chemicals and electromagnetic currents) on the one hand, and the message (the software) on the other, are not the same thing — just like the hardware and software in the computer are different things altogether. Therefore, if the message or information is an impossibility for natural selection to process, write, and implant in the right cells, natural selection is a non-starter as a viable explanation of how humans came to be the creatures we are. There must be an explanation somewhere. So, where? What? Think big — bigger! What comes to mind?

- Paul, writing almost 2,000 years ago, clearly stated an intelligent alternative to Darwin and all secular philosophies that struggle to explain our origin and obvious design…

> "For since the creation of the world God's invisible qualities,
> his eternal power and divine nature — have been clearly seen,
> being understood from what has been made,
> so that men are without excuse."[9]

A being — like an infinite, omnipotent, omniscient God — fits the bill, of course. And that's why we make the leap from the inadequate explanation called evolutionary development to a designer — to the person we call God — as the only sensible and intelligent explanation. I will "double down," as they now say in politics. All non-living beings or imagined sources that we can think of are indeed non starters.

---

[9] Romans 1:20

Paley's argument has never been answered. If upon finding a watch and examining its construction and design, we find it most reasonable to think it had a designer, why, when we see the construction and design of the human at any level of knowledge, don't we think it most reasonable that the human had a designer, too?

Power Source

At this point, the analogy of hardware and software again becomes inadequate. The computer will tell us why. It has hardware and encoded software, but it needs a power source — something outside itself — to make it work, and we need a power source, too. Power is energy, but the life that we have is more than energy. Otherwise, a battery is life and that is all we would need. We need more than a power source to effectively run this living human creature.

We plug the computer into a power outlet or connect it to a battery for it to be able to function at all. But for a human, we need a life-source. That's very different from a power source. A power source energizes; a life-source animates and makes us come truly alive in the fullest sense of the word. Definitions struggle to define the word life, and they often resort to the contrast: opposite of the word death. We need a life-source to give life to us and maintain all that the experience of life contains. We have an amazing life source that has stand-out intelligence and produces enjoyment and potential for greatness, because it empowers us to face the problems and opportunities of managing our human system under any condition thrown at us in a whole lifetime. Plugging in is as simple as establishing a trusting relationship with our designer and creator.

This life source must run successfully and repair itself without calling on a geek to analyze a problem and replace faulty parts or download needed software. It will have to deal with both the hardware and the software. Fortunately, medical doctors can repair a lot of our physical malfunctions, but they can't repair our software or the loss of life. We just don't know of an analogy that will cover all the intricate demands of a living, intelligent human system.

Standing up in the meeting of the Areopagus in Athens, Paul addressed the Athenians with these words,

> "Men of Athens! I see that in every way you are very religious. For as I walked around and observed your objects of worship, I even found an altar with this inscription: To an unknown God. Now what you worship as someone unknown, I am going to proclaim to you. The God who made the world and everything in it is the Lord of heaven and earth and does not live in temples built by hands. And he is not served by human hands, as if he needed anything, because he himself gives all men life and breath and everything else... For in him we live and move and have our being. As some of your own poets have said 'We are his children.'"[10]

Our power source is God, "... in whom we live and move and have our being."

Summary of Requirements for Human Software
One last look is at who we are and the valuable creatures who the magnificent creator God has made us to be.

---

[10] Acts 17:22ff

Our software:

- Must manufacture its own new stem cells for repair and growth, which is a daily need.

- Fights off armies of invaders, such as free radicals, that are constantly invading around the clock and sometimes, it mounts a massive attack because of the way we may have mismanaged our own system or our environment.

- Controls precise temperature levels. If our core temperature changes more than a few degrees, we are dead.

- Provides a 24/7 control center (brain) that lasts a lifetime and never sleeps. Oh, and by the way, you don't have to buy hardware and software to update every few years or replace it because of an infuriating program that malfunctions and gives up the ghost — incidentally, making you mad.

- Maintains a system that uses air, one of your needed fuel sources providing oxygen, negative ions, and other needed factors.

- Runs an around-the-clock maintenance service.

- Converts food into usable chemical substances and avoids autoimmune breakdowns — if we don't mistreat it by unwarranted stress or feed it damaging foods.

- Runs a supply program, transporting in our blood stream our nutritional needs and constantly fueling energy production for the entire body.

- Controls and runs a waste management program.

- Runs a software program that can think for itself — not robotically like a machine — with self-consciousness, providing a continual sense of who we are creatively, intelligently, ingeniously, operating just like only a human person can.

- Manages many other amazing systems that have to run with astounding precision, including a pump that lasts a lifetime and does not stop for repair, renewal, or a rest.

- Replaces damaged cells where needed. No "computer" actually creates microscopic cells and regenerates itself right before our eyes, like the human computer's life source does.

- Creates its own hardware. No computer does that. No computer reproduces its kind and nurses its offspring. If it did, Apple and Microsoft would go broke. Just one of the insurmountable obstacles to natural selection/materialism being a starter for the role of creator, or even the developer of human beings, is its inability to think and plan with purpose, plus its lack of intelligence.

- No computer does all that the human system does, writing changes to its own software continuously and, all the while — wait for it — loves you and cares for you. Oh, and this is marvelous! You will find that you will fall in love with what it has created: YOU! — primping yourself and grooming yourself and even looking in the mirror and smiling at guess who? In fact, you **must** love yourself or you will begin to malfunction.

Oh well, as you probably know, that's not all. Hopefully, it is enough to make us all think again of how naive it must be to think of the human in terms of a machine, or that we just happened and developed by evolutionary methods that lack the basic abilities to create a human being with all the demands of its life. All of the above leaves us with little reason to value ourselves and no reason to believe we have any intrinsic worth.

You and I are living creatures and should be conscious of our obvious worth. We are also intelligent and operate intelligently — except when we refuse to eat our spinach.

Don't sell your self-worth short. Don't think of yourself as the current secular philosophies and ideas (often taught by professors who want you to think you are a production of chance happenings and are a product of your environment) do: a wonderful, fine-tuned machine, or a robot that operates like a machine. NO! You have more intelligence than to believe that if you only take an honest look at who you really are.

Have the courage to believe in yourself and to be honest about who and what you are. Think of yourself in a way that lines up with the amazing facts of your biology and your own experience of who you are when you believe in your worth and don't doubt your greatness. Paul Davies, a physicist, got it so near to right when talking of what the universe has provided for the experience of the life we all enjoy. He declared his conviction, "It looks so much like a Grand Designer had figured it all out."

Nancy Pearcey,[11] who I have mentioned before, draws our attention to the fact that before Christ (that's a long time ago), people were coming to the same conclusion as Davies. Marcus Tullius Cicero, born in 106 BC and who died at 63 in 43 BC after making a name for himself, came to a brilliant observation. He was highly educated in law, oratory, philosophy, and literature (people were just as intelligent then as they are now). He wrote on the subjects of rhetoric and philosophy. Here is the quote I would invite you to ponder…

> "When we see something moved by machinery, like … a clock or many other such things, we do not doubt that these contrivances are the work of reason. When, therefore, we behold the whole compass of the heaven, moving with revolutions of marvelous velocity and … perfect regularity … how can we doubt that all this is effected, not merely by reason, but by a reason that is transcendent and divine?"

So do you get it? You and your world are creations of a great, intelligent, life-giving source, the marvels of whose intelligence are to be seen by anyone at any period of our human history. Everything Cicero said should, in the face of the overwhelming evidence of intelligent design in our universe, together with his use of irrefutable logic, be regarded as unashamedly intelligent.

Cicero and others who have come to the same conclusion knew nothing of today's intricate discoveries in biology. They were dependent on what was obvious to anyone who would take the time to observe and think. This universe and man's creative mind display the evidence of intelligent design and

---

[11] English translation of a quote from Cicero's work in *Finding Truth*, Nancy Pearcey, page 29.

urge us to the conclusion of a super-natural intelligent designer of us all.

The psalmist shows his God-given intelligence, too, in what we can now say with added confidence is a reading of the message of intelligent design. He uses these words, "The heavens declare the glory of God; the skies proclaim the work of his hands."[12] Yes, God shows his intelligence in everything around us that he has made, and we show clearly that we, too, are made in that same image because of the ability we show in our creative achievements.

Who am I? Not a machine. I am a marvel, a miracle of the creative love of God. Who am I? Words won't come near to telling the real story of how awesome a human is. The cause cannot be less than the result. Therefore, we are living creatures, showing clearly that we have been designed by a mind greater than our own. Would you say far, far, far greater?

A Side Note: Natural Selection Versus Intelligent Design

For those who want a summary, here is a brief look at the issues involved in choosing natural selection over intelligent design.

I have stated that natural selection is a form of chance. Or natural selection is, in the final analysis, chance. Some atheists who have to find a way around all you have just read try to tell us there are three alternatives that can make it to a final line-up of candidates to explain how we came to be what and who we are. These are:

---

[12] Psalm 19:1, consider also Psalm 8:3-9.

1. Chance, said by some to account for what we are and who we are,
2. A super designer, who designed humans with a purpose and an end in mind,
3. In-between these two opposite poles is evolution and its methodology, natural selection, which gets to the finish line step-by-minute step over billions of years.

Atheists agree with us that chance has no chance of explaining how a human came from the simplest form of matter to be the complex, intelligent designed being we find a human to be when we look at the human in detail. We agree. That eliminates number One.

Like we would expect, evolutionary defendants say a designer could not be responsible for our becoming what we are today. Why? A designer is not probable because such an idea is too highly unlikely. In fact, some say it is statistically improbable that a designer of such stature could exist. How did they find a way to calculate how a being with no physical elements could exist or not? They cross out number Two, also. We don't, of course.

Pause and think straight for a moment. In a debate, that's the easy way to get rid of the opposition. Just call their position unlikely. Refuse it a seat in the debate and you won't need any evidence to support your claims. There is no evidence to support their claims! But it evades the subject under discussion, begs the question "Is the design we see in the complex working detail that the designer purposefully had in mind as the end goal for a human more likely to come from a designer, or from an unintelligent, evolutionary theory called natural selection?"

Then, they add what is known in debate as a herring: the designer would have to have been designed. (A herring is chasing another issue, not directly the issue at hand[13]). It is another question, we admit, and must be answered, but not in a debate between intelligent design and natural selection.

What really happened, they say, is this: In progressive small steps over billions of years, a human evolved by natural selection. Natural selection, they maintain, is not chance; it is a succession of tiny steps toward its goal (a goal that must be unknown to a mindless process). But what is this step-by-small-step, without plan, and intelligent selection? There is no other name for it than chance. Chance selections are what happened in each minute step. What else do we call mindless happenings?

When they debate "irreducible complexity," they disregard the admission by Darwin that if it were proved that the complexity of a human was such that no operational details could be left out for it to function, his whole theory would collapse. This is precisely what has been found to be the case. When the supporters of evolution hit this obstacle, they moved to another tactic: namely, debating a straw man. (The straw man, in this case, is defining irreducible complexity in their

---

[13] Is it correct to say that a designer had to be designed? Yes, if that designer by nature had a beginning. But of course, what they must argue is not their own straw man, but the claim that the opposition presents, and that is that God is eternal. He has no beginning or end. Is it a rational claim? Yes. If he is the almighty magnificent designer of the entire universe and all that is in it, he has proved that, for him, anything is possible. In this debate we are beyond the presentation of evidence and in the world of probabilities. So if God is the creator of all things, his eternal nature is not without probability and will remain an item for a reasonable faith.

own convenient way, misrepresenting it and falsely representing the facts it presents). This is dishonest argument in any debate. Crooked thinking is just this: deliberate misrepresentations, a prime tool of sophistry.

What we have seen is that even if tiny steps were taken over billions of years, the detail we have outlined above shows that a process of natural selection cannot account for what we see in the human being, thus invalidating it as a viable option. How can something arrive at an amazing working design — intelligent and purposefully functional — if the end goal was never known or conceived? Only by chance. The numerical impossibility of it happening by chance alone removes it from even being in consideration.

Takeaway Points

- I am greater and more marvelously made than I can imagine.

- There is still so much that science will reveal about me and my amazing body, but I know enough to eliminate inadequate explanations of who I am and how I came to be.

- I am not a machine.

- My brain is a marvel of biological engineering, with chemical and electromagnetic transmission systems and so much, much more.

- I am not the result of some unintelligent, lifeless source. And if I were, it strips me of all value to know my source was nothing but and unintelligent, mindless substance. I then must conclude I am an accident in a process of evolution. And if I am no more than an accident in this universe, life is meaningless. It is an accident, too.

- To be a living human being is to be designed. Fortunately, we can even get to know our designer.

- I should take care of myself, all of myself, material and immaterial — body, mind, and soul (psyche).

- Perhaps, for simplicity, we can think this way about our mind and our brain. My mind is not the same as my brain for one obvious reason: my mind cannot be operated on by a surgeon; my brain can. One is immaterial and the other, material. One is all about ideas and thoughts (information if you like), while the other is all about taking these immaterial functions and translating them into material operations of a physical nature. We can marvel at how both function in unison in a human, as thoughts are translated into electromagnetic/chemical messages that travel through the brain, producing the actions of a physical/non-material system.

- What is life? We don't know the answer to that, so we are still searching for something we do not know. We may never know everything. But we don't need to know all there is about life. We just need to know it is an amazing gift and how to live it successfully.

- I am fearfully and wonderfully made. What else can I say?

Teaching Tools

Use the tools appropriately designed for the child's age and development.

- The parent will have to absorb this chapter first and then impact their children's minds with what it all means to them and how it makes life more worth living. All this can best be done with an understanding of the child's temperament. (See the conclusion for where to find help on temperament).

- We all can become models of straight thinking. Don't just model; draw attention to your modeling, and suggest the same for your child and others.

- These are lessons to be repeated often as the child ages so that they value themselves with ever greater meaning.

- Strive always to develop a high sense of personal worth in yourself, first, and in your children. If they don't feel good about themselves, they will fall into aberrant behavior.

- Help them feel the importance of the word *awesome* when used of human achievement and potential, and with even greater meaning when used of God. A visit to Nasa or to other displays of our human achievements will give you all you need to be impressed and to impress others with the wonder of what this amazing human can accomplish. They should come away impressed with the achievements, but also (and more importantly) with the way we have been created.

- Our culture seems not to want to think about all this, unless they reject the idea of a God, and as a result, they play loosely with false assumptions. It is called crooked thinking. Keep teaching straight thinking. Keep helping your children to identify, in particular, crooked thinking.

5 —I Am a Valuable Person. More Surprises!

We are persons. Why is it so surprising to have to point this out? Because our personhood is now being questioned and, on occasion, denied. And we are being further belittled by the crooked ways our culture has been fooled into thinking.

Parents must be aware of the way our culture's loose use of "facts" and crooked thinking is changing their children's attitudes, values, and behavior. Raising your child is not as simple as we are led to believe at times. It is the raising of *persons*. Parents will need to educate themselves, where necessary, to counter the foolish thinking that is now commonplace in our educational systems and our culture. What kind of person will your child grow up to be? Parents can influence for the better.

Want a Healthy Self-Respect —A Powerful Self-Image?

Self-respect is vital to performance, happiness, and health. I have occasion to ask many people, "Who are you?" They usually stumble at the question and give me their name and occupation. That's not who they really are. I'll often hear them express their feelings about themselves like this, "I'm not much," or "I'm no good," or "I'm just an ordinary person." How sad! How we think about ourselves *is our self-image* and, if our self-image is not healthy and strong, something is causing it. It can be that we constantly compare ourselves to others. Some think their status, occupation, the money they make, their abilities (or lack of them) define them. We are defined by how we think and feel about ourselves.

A low self-image defines us as not being all we can be. A high self-image opens the door to great performance, happiness, goodness, and health.

Therefore, think highly of who you are! Try to live with a low self-image and you will feel the pain of depression and despair, the aching void of emptiness, and the onset of worthlessness. You will cry out from the depths of your soul as you feel the emptiness and darkness of despair. This is the downward path that leads to finding no reason to live.

So, who are we? A healthy self-worth begins with a great answer to this question.

Experience this for yourself. Try to live each morning you awake, limited as you may be, but as though you are truly *made in the image of God* and a wonderful person who has endless possibilities for the day. Feel the surge of real value a belief like that gives you. Think of this, also: If the infinite God has created us and reached out to communicate with us and seek our trust and faith, is that not also a solid thought on which to build our self-worth?[14]

---

[14] If you want an excellent exposé of who God is and God's willingness and ability to reach out to us, I recommend the writings of Philosopher and Theologian, Francis Schaeffer, whose books, *The God Who Is There* and *He Is There and He Is Not Silent,* are essential reading. They make a solid argument for God as our original source and, that since he exists, he would want to communicate person-to-person with us, making personhood a firm foundation for a sense of worth.

We are going to focus on being persons in the fullest sense — persons who think, feel, make choices that determine their lives, are self-conscious beings, moral agents, and rational creatures. Believing in ourselves as persons leads to the greatest life we can live.

Where is this diminishing of our personhood coming from? A poisonous culture that actually encourages the blaming of others for our own mistakes and complaining if the state doesn't take care of us. People hold themselves in such low esteem that they don't want to be taught to fish; they want fish that others have caught handed to them. Entitlement is thought of before earning their way to meet their needs. Humans are being robbed of being the amazing productive persons they are designed to be. It is the way many of our youth are being raised, and it all starts when we lose the drive to be who we, as persons made in the image of God, really are.

First, let us understand how our value as persons is being belittled by beliefs that fall far short of what a human has demonstrated is their nature and true worth. It all starts in the way we think.

Evolution (Natural Selection) and Materialism — Robbers of Personhood

We have said a lot about the biological theory of evolution and its methodology, natural selection. As we have pointed out, evolution conveniently leaves the non-biological concerns of where life originally came from to other theories. These theories have also affected the way we think about ourselves.

121

Evolution piggybacks on a theory that actually predates it. That theory, materialism, insists everything in our universe is made of matter and that all matter can be explained in materialistic and naturalistic terms. So, to use an analogy, the two theories got married and formed a union to explain to us who and what we are.

A False Marriage of Theories (How Our Thinking Was Changed)

You will notice that the marriage turns out to be unfruitful. Here's how.

We are asked to believe…

- All is matter (simply a theory).

- Matter developed somehow into living substances and produced life (no mention of any evidence for how that happened; we are being asked to accept in on faith alone)!

- Living substances evolved from the simplest forms of life to the complex life we find in a human being (nothing but theory, again).

Evolution and Materialism are theories. We must accept their marriage as the explanation of how we came to be or we will be scorned for our lack of intelligence. Remember, to accept these theories as absolute truth is to be guilty of crooked thinking. Why? Accepting theories without demanding we follow where the evidence leads is the first reason the thinking is crooked. Second, because these theories are based on false assumptions that represent some, but not all of the facts. This is incomplete thinking.

Marrying evolution with the view that everything is matter of some kind leaves us with little room for argument, if their representation of the facts of our humanity are true and complete. We are being urged to just accept the marriage as legitimate when it is actually based on falsely representing the facts. In the old form of marriage ceremonies, it was required that the officiant ask, "If anyone can show just cause why these two should not be lawfully joined together in marriage, let him now speak, or hereafter, forever, hold his peace." The just cause that we need to speak up about it and that should nullify this marriage is that life cannot fruitfully form a relationship with a lifeless substance, such as a rock, for example. All our knowledge says this cannot happen and we know it can't. The human can cuddle the rock, but the rock will never be able to respond in kind — a meaningless marriage: no satisfying union for a human, no productive union either (no baby rocks or humans babies). The analogy is saying only one thing. Something is being misrepresented. The human in the theory of evolution is only half a human and in materialism, is no human at all. The other half of the human, our non-material half, is dismissed or denied, altering and negating our humanity.

We are asked to simply accept this unproductive marriage without noticing that inanimate substances cannot produce animate substances, and certainly not the life found in a human. We are also being asked to accept a speculation as being obviously the right answer. We should not uncritically accept speculations as fact. The rock is a lifeless form of matter, and the human is a living form of matter *plus non-matter*. Both are matter, and we are told that explanation should satisfy us. No. The human is more than matter, more than Materialism says we are. How the jump from lifeless to living matter is typically skipped over is by the use of this technique: either don't tell the whole truth, or deny some of the facts. If your child has not been shown the whole truth and left to those who tell only what they want your child to accept as truth, your child may end up confused and certainly misled?

The half-truth that both the rock and the human are matter, we are being told, is enough of the truth to eliminate the possibility of there ever having been an intelligent creator or source (non-matter) involved in the formation of our total universe where nothing but matter exists.

Crooked thinking indeed! It simply attempts to partition our minds off from the whole truth about who we are. In the process, it robs us of the most distinct differences between us and the rest of the animals: we are persons, a different order of being, not just living animate beings.

We have seen the need for both hardware and software as essential elements of life and how the marriage of evolution and materialism is a serious oversimplification of how complicated life really is. It is not straight thinking to accept an assumption as being true (only part of the truth) and build a theory on it, using this verbal sleight of hand to deceive us. This is the way crooked thinking tries to get rid of the overwhelming evidence for an intelligent designer without us noticing what is happening.

The Basic Facts of Who We Are
Let's not lose sight of some basic facts about the human race. We are all humans. We are individuals and must not agree to losing our individuality because if we do, we will lose our unique sense of worth as persons. Neither can we be herded into being defined by a social entity or group. Our identity is that of free individual persons. We find this same diminishing

of who we are at work in identity politics. Always ask, "Am I thinking with only some of the facts, or all of the facts?" Truth is found in honest representation.

So far we have discovered we are:

- Creatures belonging to an order of life that is distinct from other creatures.

- More advanced than all other creatures.

- Our identity is as individuals, not determined by a segment of society to which we belong.

- All humans are biologically male or female by gender, just like all the bisexual living creatures.

- *Most importantly,* we are *persons,* who have been intricately designed. Personhood demands a distinctive order among living creatures. It also logically calls for the acknowledgement of a designer who could fashion us as persons. Given the evidence from the astounding way we have been made, our designer must also have been more capable than we are. We are stumbling with our attempts at creating human life from scratch. Our designer did not.

- Persons share a worth that non-persons cannot feel or claim. No other animal can feel worth like we do. To rob us of the richness of our personhood is to strip us of our unique, essential value. That is devastating to all humans who know and feel they are intrinsically valuable creatures. They are being led to feel that their senses (about the reality of who they are) deceive them.

How Did We Become Persons?

We know we are persons and call ourselves persons. Where did that knowledge come from? From sensing who we are. Personhood is something we may not be able to define, but we seem to know it, anyhow. This explanation is the only one that makes sense to the human, unless otherwise influenced.

In a strange way, the fact that we are persons becomes one piece of the evidence that God is also a person. If we are persons, then it must have been a person who gave us the qualities that make us persons. A non-person would not have the ability to give what it did not, itself, have. Therefore, evolutionary theory and materialistic, naturalistic theories are disqualified in the search for an explanation to our personhood.

A person is a being that is conscious of its own nature. Personhood is the highest form of life. For a being to evolve from a lifeless beginning (an impossible idea as we have already shown), without intelligent direction and purpose to become the highest form of life would take nothing less than a miracle. Then a miracle had to be a part of our evolution. "Can't have that," they say, "the thought of miracles takes us directly back to the uncomfortable idea of a God. God forbid!"

The best and only viable explanation for where we as persons originated is in the creative work of the great intelligent Designer of our universe. The fact that we are personal beings constitutes evidence that a person was involved in our formation. This logic, and the most reasonable assumption, is a strong counter punch to the idea that we came from a non-personal cause. The admission that we humans have free will is also a fatal blow to materialism. Note the desperate attempts to explain free will in materialistic forms. All that does is provide a possible explanation in terms of brain activity, but leave untouched the real issue: what is the real cause and origin of our free will. We are indeed persons, whose origin must also be a person who had free will. To quote again what makes real sense to all the known facts of who we are, "We are made in the image of God."

Free will is one of the qualities that makes us persons. Have some evolutionist or materialist succeed in convincing us we do not have the ability to make a free choice, and, if they have incontrovertible facts, there goes our personhood. Show clearly our choice is not an automatic chemical reaction in the brain, but the free choice of a person, and the edifice of materialism also falls. That Materialism has gone to the extreme explanation, saying that an act of free will itself is only the result of automatic chemical changes in the brain, indicates their desperation to debunk the idea that there is something other than matter existing in the universe.

Of course, when they look at the brain working, they have no evidence that shows a personal decision was not made. All they have is a theory that says, before they start observing the brain in operation, what they will see happening is nothing but chemical forces at work, making a choice for us.

Tell a woman she is stunning in that one-of-a-kind, specially designed, red evening dress, and then tell her it wasn't her choice and materialists will have 50% of the world at war with them. (When their theory is fully understood, they probably will have more than 50% of the world at war with them. The other 50% will be waiting to see what happens to the materialists who exhibited such stupid courage.) You, if you don't concur with the stunning woman, will also be in deep trouble for expressing your materialistic views.

Materialists want us to think we are robotic agents, not persons. They reduce us to nothing more than a chemical factory over which we have no control and which controls our every decision and move. At the same time, we lose any sense of value we thought we had. It is maintained by some philosophers that, even though humans think they have the free will to choose, there is no place for it in their theory of how the mental system works. Therefore, it is wrong. Marvin Minsky, in *The Society of Mind,* admits that he can't give up his theory even though he knows it is false! Really? Please don't sell your reality of being a free person with the ability to make your own choices to such double talk.

Materialism, because it refuses to believe in a God, ends up amoral. No morals. They soon dishonor others and themselves. The world is no longer a safe place when morals are abandoned and God is also displaced.

Honest Evaluation

Here's the important part, immortalized in those words, "As a man thinketh in his heart, so is he."[15] Thinking in our heart is both thinking and feeling. Thinking of ourselves as fully fledged persons and feeling the same (our heart) is where we start toward a healthy self-image. We are the most worthy creatures on the face of this earth, which is no exaggeration. A healthy self-image is built on developing this belief and living confidently with it. Further, the words "made in the image of God" offer to us our highest reach to personal worth and if really believed, come with an increase of physical, mental, emotional, and spiritual vitality thrown in. We can

---

[15] I recommend the reading of *As a Man Thinketh*, by James Allen.

claim this without the pride that comes before a fall. It is the only path to the greatest sense of personal value.

Note: Not all humans behave as though they are made in the image of God. This is not a failure in how they have been made, but in their degraded behavior.

Personhood has to be our focus because of its importance to who we are. This chapter's purpose is to recover a way of thinking that transforms our lives.

What These Theories and This Thinking Have Done to Us

This next section is for clearing our heads of theories that are assumed as true, when only a part of the truth is being told to us.

Evolution, A Biological Theory

The word *theory* keeps coming up when we talk of evolution. Why? Because evolution is a belief, a theory, and not by any means is it to be regraded as a proven scientific fact. As the Encyclopedia Brittanica correctly states, "[Evolution] *is a biological theory postulating…"* (Read for "postulating," it is a proposition, *an assumed idea without sufficient factual basis to support it or give it the status of a fact. It is simply a suggestion.*) That should slow your uncritical acceptance of its reductionism. Evolution wants us to believe that, apart from our achievements, we have no value. When a person falls in love, they believe the person they love has great value, regardless of that person's achievements or lack of them.

We are expected by evolutionists to take their theory for granted as axiomatic and essential to our understanding of life, when the truth is, a theory cannot be something essential to our understanding of life. Therefore, a theory cannot claim to be indispensable.

To clear up what a theory is, let's site *Webster's Dictionary* again. I will summarize its long explanation: A theory is an imagined reality, a hypothetical set of facts, a proposition relating to nature, something taken for granted, a conjecture, speculation, or supposition. That's what a theory can claim to be.

Anything there to indicate it is fact or the whole truth? No. Therefore, we should not take it as fact. How can we know what happened billions of years ago (or even 10,000 years ago) for certain if we have no certain evidence of what took place? Wisdom says, build your beliefs on facts supported by convincing evidence — certainly, if there is overwhelming evidence. Our culture is believing theories as facts, and the result is, we are being devalued as being less than persons in our falsely placed faith. We are more than simply the byproduct of chemical happenings that occurred by chance.

To ask us to believe a theory to be true without substantial evidence is to open the door to legitimate skepticism and doubt, if not to dispensing of it altogether. Unsubstantiated theories are at least misleading when it comes to the important question of finding out who we are. Evolution's speculative assumption is defined as "all things living have their origin and owe their characteristics to other *preexisting types that are now, apparently, extinct."* The italics are to focus our attention on what, therefore, cannot be examined. This statement is not to be misconstrued as a denial of some well-substantiated archeological discoveries. Rather, of theories with less than adequate support, which have been given the status of sacred cows. Can we question the factual nature of beliefs in sacred cows? Yes, we should. They really belong to one's private beliefs — something that should be clearly understood as only beliefs, and they should in no way be presented to us or our children as facts or reality.

Otherwise intelligent people want us to believe the theory of evolution and conduct our lives as though it is true, fact, reality, something that is taboo, not to be touched by criticism. If we question it, we are mocked and made to feel inferior.[16] There is no factual basis to the belief that everything is matter or that everything in a theory is fact and reality. None!

Assumptions

As *Webster's Dictionary* (to site a reliable unbiased source) states, evolution is a "biological THEORY, postulating ...," not **proving** anything. We can't forget, theory is theory, not fact. Darwin, the author of this theory, tells how he observed minute changes in the beaks of finches under different climatic conditions. He then projected his observations of these and other changes he had observed in other studies into a theory that he called Natural Selection, *proposing* that ALL species have evolved by natural selection of what is best

---

[16] Phillip E. Johnson, a professor emeritus of the University of California at Berkley, has felt the sting from some professors at Berkley who can't believe than anyone of intelligence could not accept the theory of Evolution. I would recommend his books to you.

for their survival. It is not good thinking to project a few observations of minor adaptations into a grand theory of the way things must have happened in the development of ALL living things — especially of the formation of humans over billions of years — when that theory is wanting in its convincing explanation of its major obstacles to belief. We will visit some of these obstacles.

The "evidence" for the truth of evolution, then, lies only in the speculations of *some* scientists and philosophers — remember, not all scientist. We are being offered only speculations as to what might have happened but, of course, according to evolutionists, they "should" have happened. This kind of thinking sinks in the quicksand of its own imagination. Their plea for our faith is another way of saying, "Believe our speculations, please!"

A Theory Can't Give Us Value

Our big question to which we want an answer in this chapter is "Does it make us feel like celebrating to know that we have no intrinsic, original value, only the fleeting value we can rake up from our achievements?" Does it even make us feel we want to live, when we are told we are just an accidental happening?[17] It certainly is a downer to be told we originated in some accident found in some imagined backwater of life, as Bertrand Russel, that philosopher who was worshipped by many, would have us see our ultimate value.

---

[17] If we are a chance happening, good and evil, moral or amoral, the opposites mean nothing. Then anarchy reigns, and that never makes all the people feel good about themselves — only the leaders and those who propounded these ideas.

Such a belief dismantles any idea of personhood, too. What good is it to be a person with all the wonderful qualities of personhood, if we began as worthless creatures? What reason have we to live when our personal world has collapsed? None really, if all this is true. However, we instinctively feel we know otherwise. Do I mean that, alone, our intuition amounts to a valid theory for believing we are intelligently designed? No, because the belief in intelligent design rests not on this subjective evidence alone, but on overwhelming evidence of our design. However, being the result of an intelligent design sure makes any alternative very unattractive and undesirable. If the evidence against intelligent design were overwhelming, then we would have to believe it. It is, however, far, far from the truth. It is a theory built on false premises.

A theory can't impart value and come to our rescue — certainly not one that has no real reason to give us value. We need substantial evidence on which to ground our beliefs. One thing we know: our value is obvious to us. We are valuable creatures and we intuitively think we are valuable. In fact, we all live as though we think we are persons and have value — except of course, when our self-image plummets, which is a malfunctioning of our system. Even the proponents of evolution and materialism feel they are valuable, despite their lack of a solid assumption on which to act as though they are intrinsically valuable. Is it because of the appreciation they receive from fans that gives them this feeling? Real cause for value is established from believing we have a more promising beginning than trillions of lucky choices made by natural selection. If we are the creation of an intelligent and also personal designer, we can reasonably surmise that we were designed for a reason. The action of an infinite person who sees value in creating us, gives us our greatest reason to feel worthy.

An Intelligent Designer Can Give Intrinsic Value

At least a belief in an intelligent designer of the universe has the entire universe, with its overwhelming evidence of intelligent design, supporting the claim. The evidence elevates this belief above that of a theory to a believable fact. Intelligent design is an observation that people of different beliefs have made for over two millenniums. The consistency of our design is, for example, the belief scientists rely on every time they go to work in the lab. Call that Designer whom you will. A designer who went to the trouble of designing us as living creatures and as persons who can love makes us feel loved. To be loved is to be valued.

It means also that it is logical to think this way, because our assumption is built on the solid evidence for intelligent design. Evolution can't have the support of solid evidence or logic, because logic must begin with an assumption based on fact, not on suppositions. All such specious arguments do not bear the weight of truthful examination. A belief in an intelligent designer also has the support of revelation, with its own evidence to support it, too. But that's another story.

Embarrassment for Science

Science would be embarrassed to be represented as nothing but a mass of speculations palmed off as facts. But that is exactly what the theory of evolution has done to it. To save science from such embarrassment (remember, evolution is not science — it is only theory) insist on a theory's true nature. Evolution will remain the theory on which our culture is built until we allow the evidence of an intelligent designer to be revealed to all. That will require its admission as a valid element in our educational system. It is very sad that the theory of evolution and its devaluation of us is still the current "in vogue" understanding of who we are!

Remember, we are also told that natural selection makes minute evolutionary steps[18] because large jumps would not seem at all likely. (This claim is so obviously theory, not fact). The purpose of these minute steps, we are told, is to survive and pass on that change to the next generation, ad infinitum (more theory). So, let's imagine that this "natural wisdom" suddenly sees the need of a third eye in the back of our heads to provide greater detection of prey. Conceptually, that could be an improvement, based on a need to survive (though this obvious aid to survival was apparently missed by the evolutionary process). An extra eye would have to come about, according to the theory of evolution, by minute steps over perhaps many millions of years. What if something went wrong with one of those minute steps in simple changes that could be made to our cells, and natural selection lost its sense of direction (which it does not possess), leaving us with only half an eye in the back of our heads? Or what if something more catastrophic happened? Are we to believe that natural selection has a mind and ability to pursue a purpose over millions of years without knowing if the next minute step is the right or wrong one — just what is apparently right for survival? Natural selection is a clever choice of words, making nature (which has no such ability) sound like the new "god of creation."

---

[18] Evolution claims to be a cumulative process and this claim is the extent of its defense. We are told we should, therefore, believe that this suggestion of tiny steps proves the validity of evolution as a theory that should be accepted as fact, and as the demise of any suggestion that intelligent design has validity. There is, as you might expect, no reference to the overwhelming evidence of design in the human species and "all that has been made." See, Richard Dawkins' inadequate explanation in *The God Delusion*, page 147 in the 2008 edition.

Idol Worship of Sorts

Let's remember that this belief sounds much like the people in Bible days, who prayed to gods of wood and stone, and yet were otherwise intelligent. The prophets of old wisely laughed at their behavior and their belief in the efficacy of these idols. Perhaps that should be our appropriate reaction to the theory of evolution, as well, which claims inanimate matter possesses, by some magical fiat of nature, amazing intelligence. It is a mind-boggling exercise to believe that over many billions of years, each minute cellular step in the intricate design of a human continued successfully without the aid of intelligence and without setbacks or mishaps that sidelined the project, never losing sight of its goal and never deviating from its path. Natural selection, however, has no goal in mind.

We don't know the motivations of Darwin, of course. However, granting him credibility but also overlooking his lack of supplying us with substantial evidence for his theory, he is still not convincing, and we are left with no reason to think we are anything more than an animal. Let's be more intelligent than bowing down to a mindless theory, an idol constructed only of unsubstantiated ideas. Of course, we have no evidence or knowledge that all this was what happened over the span of billions of years. How could we know that? Then let's admit we don't know it; it is only surmising (theory). Does the theory convincingly explain how humans came to be the most advanced and complex organism in the known universe? Oh, and amazingly designed into the bargain? No! Don't buy theory based on speculation without looking the gift horse in the mouth, as the saying goes!

Please Explain

The theory of evolution leaves us with many unanswered gaps. Bear with me for one more item we are supposed to trust without skepticism. We could be excused for asking:

- How did the amazing human reproductive system come to be created by natural selection, in the first place?

- How did it leap from primitive cellular division to complex conception, birth, and nursing care, and all that these changes entail?

- What intelligence saw the need for this? Or was it just a chance happening — which makes little sense?

- And how long would it take for all of the chemistry involved to assemble itself for the human to become a working reproductive organism with an amazing way of reproducing?

- How did all this accommodate the differences in development of male and female reproductive needs, and all at the appropriate right timing?

- Did it know when a female, for her best welfare, should begin menopause and become a grandmother? Or is this also a fortuitous happening?

More: How did the human race survive as a species while it waited for the reproductive system to be fully developed, one minute step after another over perhaps millions of years, and finally become functional? Have you ever watched a new mother and her obvious value and love of her child? How did natural selection create this sense of value?

It can't, if it has no knowledge of the value of love in itself. Consider seriously that the answer to our amazing design by a very intelligent designer makes sense and is far more plausible.

Don't we feel compelled to think that if a watch shows evidence of a designer, how much more the study of the human being urges that obvious conclusion and makes it inevitable? The truth is, the origin of life and the formation of a human who senses innate value cannot be fully explained by any naturalistic, materialistic scenario. Nothing is adequate, except intelligent design and an intelligent designer — and we shall see the value that bestows on us.

How Our Culture Has Been Affected

What drives our changing culture? Thinking about ourselves differently! And why would that be happening? For reasons that appeal to a person who does not want to take responsibility for what is happening to them, or to the person who wants to blame anything or any other person for their own failures. Perhaps for reasons that appeal to those want the benefits of claiming entitlement and getting what others have without having to work for it themselves. A big attraction is the apparent freedom to do as we please with no moral restraint. Does your child have moments of thinking this way?

Evolution, Materialism, and Marxism have created the foundation for this kind of thinking. Postmodernism has popularized them. These philosophies are efforts to explain everything without reference to a divine being. These people absolutely do not want to lose their freedom to some divine being. That would mean we may have to feel responsible — to God. Avoiding this responsibility appeals to many as a convenient escape route.

Your teen likely does not understand the implications of the way the culture is thinking. They have absorbed it by osmosis from peers and teachers and, sometimes, also from parents who don't understand what it all leads to. Help them understand! Hidden in the machinations of the thinking of our current culture is an emptiness that leaves all of us without a reason to view ourselves as fundamentally valuable. A philosophy/culture that gives us value is what our Western civilization was founded upon — the Christian culture. So, Christianity is being blamed for all these "evils" it has perpetrated on the world.

We are moving from one culture to another. They are opposites in almost every way. Each proceeds from opposing views of who we are. Each culture is formed from a premise and follows the meaning of that premise to its inevitable goal.

Two Cultures Reviewed

One culture accepts the theory of evolution and the materialistic belief that everything in the universe is matter. Two broad brush strokes, conveniently removing any need to accept the evidence for intelligent design or a God. It also accepts the Marxist theories of how a culture should be governed, resulting in a communistic, totalitarian regime (the people get told what to believe and even what language is politically correct). Social justice, which does not see an individual as primarily a responsible agent, is added to the mix, but as a member of some self-styled, self-convinced, oppressed unit of society that calls for justice against its imagined oppressors. In this culture, people are often unwittingly devalued and the promises of freedom result in demands for conformity and control, not the individual freedom they thought was promised. This culture, of course, is based on secular understandings of life and our world.

Not understanding all the implications of these beliefs, people willingly buy into it for the personal benefits that are deceptively sold to them. Ultimately, if these beliefs are carried to their end results: people become oppressed and find they cannot live happily without personal freedom and the value that being a free person gives them.

The second culture will be the one that grants to the individual the highest sense of personal worth — a worth that comes from our Designer and Creator in whose image we are made. This culture believes we have been endowed with the gift of free choice and are also responsible beings who live in a world where truth and falsehood, right and wrong guide our lives. In this world, we are called to create the most satisfying and rewarding way to live, striving toward achievement and success for ourselves and others. We are, by our choices, creators and the responsible agents of our lives. It is this culture that is losing ground — fast — in an all out effort to control the way people think.

Culture One
The True Premise Behind the Culture:
We are not the result of some intelligent and personal source. We are material beings and that is all. We are the result of an evolutionary process that somehow lead us from being inanimate to being a living being. This inanimate force (natural selection) produced all living things without having any intelligence, mind, goal, or purpose, and all this does not

give us pause for concern. Because there is nothing but matter in this universe, we are self-deceived if we think that spiritual and non-material explanations exist.

The Outcome of the Premise for a Teen — Does It Ring True to You?

When I think of who I am, I think I make decisions. But in reality, I'm told, I don't and that the chemicals and forces in my brain make my choices for me. My brain actually presents me with these choices and makes me feel they are mine. I feel relieved! I don't have to go on a guilt trip, feeling responsible for all I do. I can do what I want and what is right for me doesn't have to be right for other people, although I feel they should think and act like me. Therefore, it occasionally occurs to me that I may be a kind of robot, controlled by my physical brain. But my way of thinking is "So be it! Whatever!" I'm OK with being blasé about it, too, because it lets me off the hook of being all the time concerned about having to think of how my actions affect others.

When my parents keep at me about being more responsible and doing what they think is right, I think they are trying to pressure me into doing what they want me to do for their benefit.

Because I don't have to report to God, as they try to remind me I will, I can do what I want. Where are they coming from? What is right or wrong is my choice! Get it? I like that. It's a kind of neat way of thumbing my nose at the world! At times its all confusing to me because I do feel guilty if I hurt someone I care about.

I don't care about everyone or even my parents, at times. I care about the ones that think like me.

The way I saw it in a lecture the other day is, I am totally and always a part of this mindless process called ongoing natural selection. I don't understand it, but that's kind of scary. What is this ongoing natural selection going to do to us humans next? Don't get me wrong; I'm really not concerned. I probably won't be here when that happens anyway.

My parents often hammer me about being consistent. The reason seems clear to me, because I think to be consistent means I am establishing a precedent or a reputation, and that will, in a kind of way, constrict my absolute freedom to be who I want to be in the moment. I could look at it this way: inconsistency benefits me because when I want to change my behavior, there is nothing — not even my own past behavior — that can try to limit or influence what I do. I am morally and absolutely free! That's real living! Free to lie (that's helpful), steal, and butcher whoever gets in my way. (Of course, in what they call my better moments, I don't think I would do that). I am also free to be altruistic and magnanimous (that's a big word for me). My parents think its good, somehow. But why? Why be good? I hope my brain makes the right choice for me. But then again, since I have no moral standards, there can't be a right and a wrong for me. Right? I'll admit, I'm a little uneasy about this. What if I don't want what my impulses choose for me? Or is that possible? What if I want to change someday? Explain that to me.

Following this absolute freedom idea, I think Stalin, Hitler, and Isis had a point — although I would never let my parents feel I think that. To be totally free, they had to suppress other people so they wouldn't get in their way. My mind went wild and free the other day. I was thinking something like this… "I will have to become the ultimate authority over all other people in the world. That power is a great feeling and who's to say it is wrong for me? I'll seek power — the power to make rules and laws and execute them at whatever cost to me or to others. In quest of this power, I will become, in the eyes of most, a brutal dictator, and people will serve me out of fear. I will constantly have to watch my back. I know that. As long there is another person who will not obey me, I will need to go to bed at night with an armed guard. In this technological age, I will also need the protection of amazing weaponry that continually searches land, sea, and sky for any indication of a suspicious movement. It just occurred to me, I can see why Hitler was paranoid? It's a byproduct of his belief that he had to be in control. This seemed to be the price for the total freedom he wanted."

Here I am again, being crazy. Im just trying to dream of the freedom I want. Again, excuse my ramblings, but I'm just going on what I have been taught in university, and surely they know what they are talking about. Right? My parents wanted me to go to university.

Well, I think we all should be equal and those who are rich should share all they have with the likes of us who don't have what they have. All this talk of entitlement has a point. Why should I suffer when others rip me off, making money off me every time I pay for something? If the world is fair, people like me would be taken care of. I am simply unfortunate.

But here's the other side of my mind: I'm feeling so empty and disconnected to my world and, of course, others. What happened to the real me, the one I am familiar with, who makes my own choices and is sensitive to good and bad? At times, I really want my old me back. I want to make my own decisions and feel like I felt before I was told to think all this about myself. It makes me feel less than who I felt I was before.

Teenager, does the outcome of this premise sound exciting to you? Would you prefer to live as though you are an intelligent person with a brain and a mind of your own? You and I actually think we make our own choices, don't we? We live as though we do every day, true? And it feels right, like its right for us to think this way about ourselves. So, it's natural to think as though we are not the evolution of some mindless, unintelligent, lifeless piece of matter, isn't it? Would you like to live in a society where everyone refuses to take responsibility and says, "Don't blame me. My brain made me do it"? No, thank you!

Welcome to Culture One, a logical and consistent result of a mindless and unintelligent evolutionary process that is nothing but matter at work. What we think does matter, doesn't it?

Reread this section, because it may flag you about how your child (or you) understands the world we live in. Mark what you see needs to be addressed for the ultimate good of your child.

Culture Two

The True Premise Behind the Culture:
All humans are the result of an intelligent person (our designer) who, with intent, purpose, and a clear goal in mind, made us in his own image.

The Outcome of the Premise for a Teen — Does This Sound Better?

> *When I think of who I am I sense that I have some sort of natural value. My source, we could say, is on record as loving and approving of what he did in making me. Feeling this value, I sense the equal value that all others must have, too. This shared value gives me strong feelings of respect for others. It creates a bond with others that is not dependent on their behavior. It also forms the basis for the love I have for all people — but for some more particularly than others (especially the one I have fallen in love with). My inherent value gives me a sense of worth that no one can take from me. It also makes sense of The Golden Rule, "Do to others as you would have them do to you," which is a logical behavioral result of this premise.*

> *My source becomes my natural authority as to how I can best live this life and achieve the greatest enjoyment from it. My source should know this, since*

he designed me and knows how I operate. When I follow my source's "rules" for living, I feel they are right for me. They extract the best out of me and offer the best guidance for my life on this earth with others. I love myself because I feel I am valuable and this feeling of value uplifts my spirit. All this helps me discover the truth in the words "love never fails." This is a culture not built on tolerance, but on something far greater — on love. It just takes me a little thought to realize how love beats tolerance any day.

Because I know there is such a thing as right and wrong, it makes sense that since no one is perfect, justice and mercy are also a natural outcome for this premise. That means that personal responsibility for our actions is needed to assure the best for everyone. This is a culture that honors all people equally and seeks the right and the good for all, not just some. For those who do wrong, there is justice and mercy, whichever is warranted. Friendships can freely develop in this culture and it is where true love thrives. Love is the greatest feeling of all. It is the heart and soul of a true bonding and is the way to a relationship that is heavenly. I'm sorry if you are tightly closed to all things belonging to a human or the Divine Spirit, but I hope you will unlock your mind and not fight the idea that your first and lasting value comes from Who made you.

I also know I make free choices. I know it is me that chooses, and my choices are the making of my life. This is because all my choices bring consequences and I must own my part in them. I must seek to grow in my ability to make even better choices. I must be consistent or I am not recognizing the challenge I have to behave for the good of all and for the honor of what is good — always. I am also not building an honorable character for myself if I don't.

I recognize the horrible evil of using my gift of free choice to destroy others and to misrepresent the truth. Without truth, this culture would fall apart, and Culture One will too. Lying in this culture is a grave crime against the very culture itself — an action against the very culture that seeks to protect me. Strange that everyone seems to think lying to them is punishable, but their lying to others is permissible. They usually excuse it, if their goal is some ideology or religious belief that, to them, justifies the idea. In this culture the goal never justifies the means.

I wake every day with a purpose, not solely for some achievement I have in mind but for being the person I know myself to be. I enjoy the sense of fulfillment such a purpose in life gives me. I sense the warming pride of becoming more like my source and more like the good in me wants me to be.

Because of knowing right and wrong, but being imperfect myself, I seek the mercy and forgiveness of my Creator-source and offer it, also, to all who offend against me. All this while everyone, including me, must face the consequences of our actions.

I have a reason to live, and I choose to live in this culture and promote its life here on this earth so we all can live in love and unity. It's the only way we can find unity with personal freedom also intact. To do so recognizes who I am proud to be and become: a valued person, not a production of some inanimate, mindless source. I am the result of my loving Designer, Creator God.

Welcome to Culture Two, a logical and consistent outcome of its premise and the very opposite of Culture One's premise.

Persons, Not Just Animals

Who am I? I am the most advanced creature in the animal kingdom! We should have no argument over that. But I am more than just an advanced animal. I am a person in the fullest sense of the word.

Is being a person part of being a human? Yes, we probably think so — all of us. Well, not all. For evolutionists and materialists, it is hard to make evolutionary sense of a human being as a person. It's easy to see that we have evolved as individuals. Being a person, however, is something more than just being an advanced animal or an individual. The theory of evolution stumbles to explain where personhood came from. It can't do so with any real sense. We see humans develop the qualities of personhood progressively, all the way from conception to death. This is because being a person means being able to think and feel, along with a lot of other things we will examine. These things, we get better at as we age.

It is surprising to many people that our being a person is even an issue that is being challenged these days. But it is. Here's one example of how it is being challenged.

✶ ✶ ✶ ✶ ✶

A Hot Debate Around Personhood

The word *person* is currently at the heart of the abortion debate. When is a human a person? You may be excused if you take a second look at those words to see if you read them correctly. We have always thought a human is a person and a person is a human being, haven't we? For most of us, yes, a human is a person. But this is not true for all, as we have already seen.

The word person is defined differently. The first definition of the word person in *Webster's Third New International Dictionary* reads, "An individual human being." The eighth definition reads that a person is a being with "conscious apprehension … rationality, and a moral sense." Person, in the last definition, is being defined by its characteristics, not by the nature it possess.

Defining a person by their characteristics and not their nature has engendered the hot debate over when it is legal or right to abort a fetus. Abortion arguments are now using the terms "human being" and "person" to refer to the fetus at different stages of development. Science confirms the fact that, at conception, the tiny fetus is a human being, because it possesses human DNA — case closed, you might think.

But the pro-choice movement argues, although that may be the case, the fetus is not yet a person. It has not shown the characteristics of being a person yet — namely, using the *Webster's* eighth definition, "The characteristics of

149

personhood, conscious apprehension, rationality, and moral sense." They avoid the first definition that *Webster's* uses, which is the basic definition of personhood. It is certainly hard to argue that at conception, the fetus shows signs of conscious apprehension, rationality, and a moral sense.

It also appears this pro choice argument has not as yet been finally settled, either. This is because there is no agreement among the pro-choice advocates as to when the fetus, or even the child after birth, becomes a person. Some say in the first trimester; some, the second; some, the third; and some, not until after toddlerhood. The age at which a human being becomes a person appears to be an issue that may never be resolved. The reason is, there is no clear evidence when the characteristics of personhood become evident, or evident enough, in a developing human being to be conclusively a person. Some adults are still not showing clear rationality or moral sense. Clearly the development of personhood is a process.

The question becomes, if a human being is not showing conscious apprehension, rationality, and moral sense, are they a person? The pro-choice proponents argue that a mere human being does not have the basic rights that a person has and, therefore, a person has greater rights than a human being. When is a human a human is age definable: we are human beings at conception — no argument about that. When is a person a person — when judged by the indisputable presence of all the characteristics of personhood — cannot be definable by an age at which it can be said to be conclusively true. As someone has quipped, " I know some adults who don't seem to show a well developed rationality and moral sense. Perhaps they are not persons yet."

If the fetus is not a person, then it is not legally under the protections persons seem to be accorded by the law. Hence, the legal fight. What a mess! When the characteristics that a creature displays define it more than what it is by nature (i.e., a person is a human being), we are accepting that a progressive development of characteristic features defines us more than biological facts. This is never how we define what a wolf or a chameleon is. All creatures are defined by what they are by nature. Why not humans? Motivations for all this splitting of terms are probably a partial reason for the ongoing debate. Could it also be that the legal use of terms is not the criterion on which the questions surrounding abortion are to be solved. Is the nature of the individual more important than the characteristics he/she show and their legal status?

The argument has been clearly moved from what it takes to be a human to what it is to be a person. What's the difference? Does what we are as humans not also contain in embryo the characteristics that, as a person, we will progressively show? It's true of the acorn which is, by nature, a tree. The characteristics all creatures show differ at different ages.

Another question arises. Why is it insufficient to be seen as only a human being? The argument of the pro-life supporters also circles around the fact that, as the fully developed tree is latent in the seed, so the fully developed human and fully developed person is latent in the tiny embryo at conception. It seems rather false to say a human is not a person until some age that is not agreed upon, when the consequences of such disagreements are disastrous. It is okay to kill a human, but not a person? Really?

✳ ✳ ✳ ✳ ✳

The direction of the current culture is to not just reduce the meaning of being a person (characteristics, not nature), but also to reduce the worth of being a human from being a person to simply an advanced animal. That better fits the popular theory of evolution and the philosophy of materialism.

How does it better fit the theory of evolution?

- By refusing to admit the credence of how humans have always thought of themselves — as persons and a unique order among the animals.

- By not having to explain how a creature that has evolved, in the first place, from lifeless matter to being a living being must have happened.

- By not having to explain how humans made the jump from being an animal to being a person.

These bumps (and more) in the road to making evolution make sense to the thoughtful mind are best avoided than explained for the evolutionist. To believe we are simply advanced animals is the logical conclusion of both the evolutionist and materialist ways of thinking (based on theories — not facts — and on false assumptions). Avoidance means they do not have to explain the non-material elements of the human and our daily experience of them.

Without personhood (a non-material distinction), we have no greater worth than an animal and, therefore, can be seen as simply an advanced animal. So, being a person is the battleground of those who oppose intelligent design and a Designer, whether they understand it or not. That we are persons in the fullest sense is supported by straight thinking and solid evidence. The evidence for humans being persons needs to be presented.

What Makes a Human a Person?
Nature and Characteristics

In this section you will find the subjects of great concern challenging you to greatness or for parenting your child. We will focus on the nature and characteristics of a person, which is all important to becoming a healthy person whose self-esteem will aid him/her for a lifetime.

Language Has Something to Say About Personhood

Our language begins the psychological evidence. It suggests a universal experience of mankind's personhood. We have felt the need to form words to differentiate between persons and things and between persons and animals — words like some*one* and some*thing*. Lovers of animals break with grammar and call their pets he or she. Nothing wrong with that sentiment. However, we have always felt the need of personal nouns and pronouns when we talk of ourselves — he or she, not it. How we think is revealed in how we talk, which suggests we have always sensed a difference of nature between us and all other creatures. That difference is personhood.

We are a *someone* and we know it. We are not a some*thing*, and we react with disgust when so addressed! Incidentally, our Creator and Designer can be referred to as he or she (male or female) because both male and female are made in

God's image. It is equally accurate to say female and male because, being equal, it does not matter which comes first. I like the thought that when someone insists on being addressed as a person, they are also declaring what they intuitively feel about themselves. We can't suddenly dismiss this persistent notion. However we came to be, we surely cannot be less than what we know and experience of ourselves daily, can we? It is a light that shines within. All theorists, take note.

To reduce our feelings of personhood to being born of chance — something less than a person or just a machine made of human cells — would shout the fact that we have cultivated and lived a lie (because of self-deception) over all of known human history. We certainly need more than a postmodern belief to persuade all of us to accept a demeaning demotion to something less than a person, less than what we have always thought ourselves to be.

Of course, it is reasonable to believe there is a motivation behind such a demotion that so dramatically alters our worth and sense of value. The motivation lies at the feet of a wholesale sellout to evolutionary theory and to materialism. If God is dead, then our value died with him too. And if this demotion is believed, the human race will have demoted themselves. For what good? Strangely, this is what some of the advocates of this reductionist way of thinking want us to believe is the real truth. But they don't act as though they believe it. Skeptically, we ask, "Why do they still go on showing their belief in their own intrinsic value?" They do so as though we don't notice their inconsistency.

It's not some of us, but all of us — including our ancestors — who have believed that what we sense is the truth about ourselves is emphatically who we are. The reductionists' inconsistency hands out the pink slips to all of us, banished by nothing else but their ravings, and they stand there holding the warrants for their crime of indignity against themselves as we smile knowingly of their folly. Yes, not one of those who tell us we are less than a true person live as though they are less than a true person. Until these advocates consistently practice what they preach, in all aspects and matters of their lives, we do not need to listen to them. The truth is, they are demonstrating to us that we can't live satisfyingly the way they believe, anyway. If they are perceptive of their own feelings, they must believe deep inside what they say is a lie. What they do is hypocritical.

History has well documented the mistake of robbing people of their sense of dignity and true worth. Civilizations have self-destructed when dignity for all people and the value that morals and beliefs give us are squandered. The Roman Empire is one example of this decay from within. Take away our sense of worth (seen in the loss of moral values) and the human creature acts like they are no more than an animal. This is an argument used in Genesis 9:6 (very ancient literature). Paraphrasing, it says: murder is forbidden, based on the fact that we are extremely worthy beings who are made in God's image. Who am I? I am both a more advanced creature than the other animals and, also, I am of a different order. I am a person!

Children Have Not Missed the Obvious, Either
Perhaps it is humiliating to admit that children have a sense of their own importance and dignity, even if we have lost ours. Children fight to defend their self-worth. From their earliest days, they have instinctively felt who they are. It has been observed by psychologists that children universally seem to prefer to think of other humans — and even their cherished

pets — as having an intelligent and intentional creator. That's quite an admission from the field of psychology.

However, unfortunately, the child grows up and changes their feelings about themselves only when influenced by adults who feel they have arrived at a better understanding — namely, we came from an unintelligent source and we are really just advanced animals or machines built of human cells. Again, no one lives that way. The real question is, do we want to discard what we intuitively know of ourselves for some theory that has been generated in an effort to suppress the idea of an intelligent designer?

They suppress the all-too-obvious truth. It is remarkable that almost 2,000 years ago, Paul wrote these words:

> "His [God's] invisible attributes, namely his eternal power and divine nature, have been clearly perceived, ever since the creation of the world, in the things that have been made, so that men are without excuse."[19]

He also noted that in suppressing the knowledge of the truth, people don't see fit to acknowledge God[20] — a very needed insight into the condition of the minds of those who must, at all costs, reject the idea of a divine intelligence behind the forming of the universe. Without conscience or sense, this way of thinking trashes our ultimate value of ourselves.

---

[19] Romans 1:18.

[20] Romans 1:28.

Nature

Nature speaks loud and clear. *Webster's Third New International Dictionary, Unabridged* cites eight definitions for the meaning of the word person. The eighth will be our focus in the pages ahead. But let us remember what the first does not allow us to forget: we are persons, first and foremost, by virtue of our *nature* as human beings.

Our nature is that of intelligent, self-conscious creatures. Our intricate and irreducible design indicates we come from the hand of an intelligent personal source and we exhibit a nature of a higher order, the highest order in all of the known universe. To say we are simply more advanced than all the other animals and our, supposed, nearest cousin is the ape is a shabby way of trying to hide reference to our true nature. Our purposeful design is stamped all over the way we feel and function as humans, not in any way mistaken for the emotions and behavior of the other animals.

Exceptions do exist among humans who use their free will to act depraved and "animal like," raw in tooth and claw, at times. They belittle themselves, not the order of homo-sapiens (*homo*, man; *sapiens*, the wise ones), which term has been accepted as true of us without a feeling of pride, but with a sense of realism. Now, it is being rejected as inaccurate by those who feel the need to call us simply "advanced human animals." It is as a result of an intuitive sense that we naturally think of ourselves as of the order of persons, and we claim to be persons. Our personhood is a given quality, not the result of being more advanced, and not an achieved status due to what is obvious: our superior mind/brain and astonishing achievements.

We are person's in the fullest sense of the word. That sense is of being of a different order, a different nature — correctly called our human nature, not our animal nature. Our personhood derives from our source who, logically, must also be a person.

Characteristics

As the eight definition in *Webster's Dictionary* reminds us, even though we are creatures of a higher order, we display the features of that order. The list that *Webster's* cites is not all of the features of personhood, but it lists some major items: conscious apprehension, rationality, and moral sense. We will, however, attempt a more complete list of characteristics.

Parents need to focus on each characteristic and increase the awareness and appropriate skills of each in themselves and their children. This is what it is, in a practical sense, to be a person.

1. We Are Creatures That Think:
Perhaps a memorable statement of this feature of being a person comes from the story of Descartes (a reference we have referenced but will now tell in full) and the time he spent in his oven[21].

In the winter of 1619-1620, he tells us, he climbed into his oven (this story sounds as though it won't end well) to spend a whole day in meditation. (What a place to meditate!) Upon

---

[21] Descartes was a famous French philosopher who was seeking to find the one truth that could be the foundation on which to base all his thinking. He tells this story in his book *Discourse on Method,* written in 1637 AD.

entering, he thought his philosophy was only half-baked. When he exited, he tells us his thinking was fully baked. He had thought himself to the conclusion of what he believed was the basis for the real truth about us. He had resolved, as he entered the oven, never to accept anything as true that he did not believe was really true. (We could have pursued the same procedure outside the oven and been less nervous!)

Anything that he doubted, he excluded as untrue. He arrived at one truth about himself that he did not doubt. Because he had doubts, he reasoned that he must be thinking. So he formulated his famous dictum "I think. Therefore I am." Well, all of us think, and thinking rationally is a feature of being a person. But an animal shows signs of rudimentary thinking, too. So let's make that more definitive of us. If we think abstractly, for example, we sit on a bench and contemplate the beauty of a sunset; or we think about love and what really makes love, love; or we dream up complicated plans and strategies that are so far beyond an animal's capability that it cannot be called simply an advance on animal thinking. This is thinking that belongs to another world of intelligent activity. This is the thinking of a person. This kind of thinking becomes one distinguishable element that makes a person a person.

Because we think, it is evidence that our source, also, can think abstractly, logically, and in all the ways we humans use thinking to solve our problems and meet our challenges. The evidence from what humans have been able to accomplish and from an examination of their tiny cells to the mighty planets of our universe, places the thinking of our designer in another world above that of our own. A non-thinking source cannot be the source of a person who thinks, unless you believe in unproven evolutionary leaps that take on the character of magic at work. I simply can't put my faith in unsupported magical leaps.

It is evident that thinking like humans can think gives meaning and definition to being a person. It elevates persons to levels of value that cannot be dreamed of for lesser creatures. To think as a human can think also reveals the profound nature of what it is to be of the order of a person. "As a man thinketh … so is he."[22] Using thought, we can also arrive at this reasonable conclusion: the potential for being a person must have been latently existent at conception, since it emerges in the infant without required training and becomes a significant indicator of who we are. Just as all the characteristics of the tree are latent in its seed, so it was latent in the embryo. Without this characteristic, we would be seen as just another living creature. The clear evidence is, we are more and we are different.

It has been said that if a person can think and devises an argument against the existence of God, they have just provided evidence of his existence and his being the source of our existence, too.

Thinking is also a skill that can be trained. It can be used properly or improperly. Think of straight and crooked thinking as we outlined it in Chapter One. Parents, in developing that little person in your charge, this is challenge number one.

2. We Feel and Have Emotions:

Our thoughts are often saturated with emotions. It is, perhaps, impossible to separate emotion and reason in the mental activity of what is happening in the moment. Our

---

[22] Proverbs 23:7 AV.

thoughts contain emotions and our emotions take on the form of thoughts. Research has shown that we cannot think without some emotional reaction taking place in us. Sometimes, that mental reaction is small; sometimes, volcanic, changing the landscape of our lives. A lack of emotion can have equally damaging or beneficial results. It depends on the nature of the emotion. We often define ourselves with our emotions.

We also feel we cannot do without them. To have no emotion is simply not possible. Emotion is a part of who we are as persons. We have emotions when we eating exercise. In fact, all the time, our emotions are recording a state of existence from calm to exuberance, from hate to love, or pleasure to anger. Emotions are the driving force in our lives and they are where our motivations are born and live.

Emotions express our personhood in unique ways. The newborn baby shows emotion — of which we become very much aware as parents. It seems also to exist in the fetus. All the way through our lives, emotions are us. Just as we are not only thinkers, we are not only feelers. The two can never be divorced. How we control our emotions (and we can) further differentiates who we are as persons.

Our emotions are more complex than our rational thoughts, require more management, and can be managed and felt by us in a way other animals can't experience. Like the other animals, we are living creatures; but we are also living persons. Persons experience emotions with fine definition, sensing them in relation to both themselves and others and discovering the vast meanings of life in them. Some would fly to the argument and say it is just that we feel to a greater degree than the other animals. Although that argument is correct as far as it goes, it falls far short of the leap to this other world of experience that humans testify to with their emotions. Our emotions are interwoven with our personalities because we experience them through who we uniquely are and define ourselves to be and become. Emotional experiences are never seen cloned in the feelings of another person. They belong to the person we are.

Take love, for an example of emotion's complexity when experienced by a person.

- Consider, with an open mind, how the words below describe an experience far different from an animal's experience of love.

- Consider that each word of this poem is understood in different shades of meaning, all finely engineered by our temperament and experiences.

- Consider how each phrase expresses new dimensions of life and impacts that dimension.

"Love is patient,
Love is kind.
It does not envy,
It does not boast,
It is not proud.
It is not rude,
It is not self seeking,
It is not easily angered,
It keeps no record of wrongs.
Love does not delight in evil,
But rejoices in the truth.
Love always trusts,
Always hopes,

Always perseveres.
Love never fails."[23]

These words are drawn from a description of what our source, the God of love, emotionally finds so fulfilling and desirable in his relationships with us. It is the way he manifests himself. Made in that image, this is the love we are urged to experience, too, though it is at times poorly replicated in us.

Now consider the different order of experience and meaning a human person achieves from the faint shadow of love we see in other living creatures. "Made in God's image" imparts to us a different nature, not just a greater degree of emotion. Whenever we love and feel the need of love, we are proving to ourselves the obvious connection we have with an image that is distinct from that of other living creatures. It is emotion enriched by personhood and personhood enriched by emotion.

Our emotions are managed by our complex rational thoughts and, therefore, we can infuse them with rational concepts and decisions to a degree no other animal can begin to experience. Persons feel and emote like only persons can. This element of our nature can be the most wonderful thing about us, or the most damaging. A person's emotions cannot be equated to a principle or a force of nature, either.

Because we feel and possess a wide range of complex emotions that enrich our lives, we ask, where did all this come from? Did the most complex feature in our makeup evolve? And if so, what directed its evolution? Since purpose is written all over our experience of emotions — we know we

---

23 1Corinthians 13:4-8, New International Version

have them for a reason. It's not sufficient to say our emotions evolved from felt needs. Our emotions shout design, purpose, intelligent function. We cannot avoid the conclusion that it must either be that natural selection has intelligence, purpose, and is a fabulous designer, far beyond what the theory of natural selection will allow. Or there is an intelligent personal Designer behind their creation. God, also, must have emotions like us — in fact, emotions that must exceed ours. We can reasonably surmise that he has a greater reservoir of emotional responses than we do, since he loves us all and loves with a love far greater than ours. He loves us, even when we abuse and ignore him and curse him. However, unlike our love, his is not stained with selfish motives and imperfections.

So, who am I? I am a person with the characteristic that we find in all human persons: complex emotions. By nature, my emotions show themselves as different in so many ways from other animals. I must learn to manage this gift, and because of all the facets of what it means to be a person (and I am a person), I can.

3. We Can Determine Our Own Actions

This is not the same as saying we can act and, therefore, we are persons; we can decide and, in the process, thoughtfully plan and fashion our own futures and lives — a universally acknowledged truth. However, in our present culture, our future is being conditioned more by our social grouping than our individual decisions. Are we going to accept that this social identity is the best future for society and ourselves? We are persons who make our own decisions. We can act according to our desires and contrary to our desires, having the ability to self control, to reward ourselves, or deny ourselves, and all with conscious intent and the use of rational thought.

We can decide to do what we want to do and, also, not to do what we want to do, following complex, ever-changing desires and even fleeting wishes. We know the difference between a wish and an urge. We can weigh evidence and make decisions based on facts or simply on feelings. Again, we know the difference. Actions are the natural outcome of our thoughts and feelings. Deciding can become a very complex action or a knee jerk reaction, thoughtful or thoughtless. And all bring responsibility to our decisions. By our actions, we determine and shape our lives.

This, again, provides evidence that because we can make decisions, so must the source who created us. It is, yet another window into who God is and who we are. Who we are constitutes evidence of who our source is. The very first descriptions of God are of a God of decisive action. A God who is actually **in** action.

The key factor here in our nature as persons is the individuality of self-conscious determination and choice that we display. We don't all react to the same circumstances in the same way. There is an individual stamp on our actions that says, "This is me." Action does not exist in an inanimate source or principle; nor does self-determination, choice, and complex decision making evolve from it. The action of an animate source is not of the same kind. Our actions can arise out of very complex mental proceedings or influences directed by abstract beliefs and values pertaining to who we want to become. Each time we think and understand who we are, we also come up with evidence of who and what our source is.

4. We Are Self-Conscious Beings

Because we are conscious beings, we are also evidence that our intelligent source is a conscious being (a cause cannot be of a lesser nature than the result it produces). Look at yourself; think about yourself. Are you simply a force with no self-consciousness, like the wind or the other forces of nature? Do you see yourself without life or without the feelings and experience that a self-conscious soul emits? Do you fulfill your intrinsic nature's longings with the lack of self-reflection of a sprouting seed? As nature automatically sets its course, that seed becomes a beautiful tree, and every year, it multiplies. But it has no understanding of itself. It cannot step outside of itself and, with objective plans, design something other than itself.

The tree doesn't drive down to the local bank and withdraw some cash. There is, obviously, something more about us. We are consciously aware of ourselves, our world, our purpose, and our meaning in life, just like our source would have to experience. If natural selection were our source, we would be like the tree and no more. We tower above the unconscious, and yet amazing, forces of nature.

Because at any moment, we are conscious of who we are, how we look, how we are appreciated by others, and how we are coming across to others, does that not tell us we are self-conscious beings of a different order than other living beings? These things and more constitute a self-conscious person. It is hard to think of who we are as persons without consciousness coming up at every turn of our lives.

But you may not, as yet, have understood that consciousness has no place in the popular theories of our supposed evolution. They want us to believe that our mind, ideas, emotions, and even our sense of self-consciousness are all the automatic result of chemical or electromagnetic reactions in our brain or some such solely physical functions. No honest search for or consideration of a non-material cause is even entertained. The obvious design in every part of us, down to the minutest operation of a tiny cell, calls loudly for consideration of such immaterial things as purpose, intelligence, and irreducible design. This path of discovery of who we are has been labeled taboo by evolutionists and materialists alike.

Some scientists, steeped in materialism, are struggling to find a "physical cause" for our consciousness. But please, even if they discovered how self-consciousness functions on the physical level and, maybe, even where self-conscious feelings are located in the brain, *function is not cause*. The cause of our self-consciousness is not likely to be discovered due to the etherial nature of self-consciousness. It is found in the etherial psyche. The same goes for free will and all the other activities of our minds.

Natural selection actually offers a cause: namely, everything about us is a result of nature having given us what we need at every stage of our development to meet our needs, and here we are, as we are. This is an inadequate answer, to be more than generous. For nature to know what we need amounts to the use of intelligence, which is nowhere to be found in the theory of natural selection. If admitted, that would destroy the theory. The real cause is an intelligent designer, obvious in the overwhelming evidence of design and purposeful intelligence we find all the way down to the cellular level of our being. The logical and most obvious cause is rejected outright because it hurts these self-limited thinkers to even think about it. Like Nietzsche, it makes them angry to think of it.

Physics and chemistry have been responsible for wonderful discoveries, but to draw the conclusion that they explain everything about us is to close our minds to all the facts that we experience daily and that form our reality. Discovering how something operates in the brain is a far cry from finding its cause. The physical actions and reactions of our chemistry and electromagnetic impulses are not who we are. They are how our cells and physical make up operate.

We must conclude that the nature of self-consciousness in persons makes them stand apart in their nature from all other creatures. Self-consciousness is at the heart of what it is to be a person.

Perhaps the most foolish and desperate idea that has been hoisted upon our students is that consciousness does not exist; it is an illusion. If it is, I am an illusion too. And yes, some philosophers have, with straight faces, promoted that idea as being the absolute truth about who we are. Strange that our experience of who we are scoffs at that conclusion, isn't it? The rationale for this absurd reasoning, as you might expect, goes like this: if nothing in the physical world can explain consciousness, then it must not exist; it must be an illusion.

Note the crooked thinking. It starts with an assumption that consciousness can't be explained in terms of physical matter. So far, the assumption is correct. Consciousness can't be explained in physical terms. But the assumption then draws an unwarranted, illogical conclusion: therefore, consciousness does not exist.

All who think physical matter is all there is, have with this conclusion conveniently eliminated from discussion a part of the world we all know exists. We immerse ourselves in this non-material world daily and live as though it exists, loving and experiencing our self-consciousness as a reality and what makes us experience our reality. The world of the non-material is the world of the mind, will, spirit, soul/psyche, spiritual experiences, and *consciousness* itself.

5. We Exhibit a Moral Sense

Websters Dictionary reminds us that having a moral sense is also a feature of personhood. It did not escape the minds of those who define the meanings of our language. Humans have a conscience and a sense of duty, responsibility, and a natural sense of right and wrong. It makes real sense to understand this moral sense of right and wrong as being part of our human nature, part of being a person. All people of all races and cultures have it. It results in the formation of delicacies like manners, diplomacy, the development of values, and is part of all that we feel and think. Its universality, alone, awards it a place among the characteristics of the highest form of life known in this universe: a person.

A lack of morals lies at the very core of all evil and all disparagement of others. Without morality, a society malfunctions and eventually destroys itself. Even the most cherished of emotions, love, is rotten to the core without some sense of goodness and moral concern for the other person.

6. Reason, Logic, and Common Sense

We must take into account the evidence of who we instinctively know ourselves to be at our best: logical creatures, as Aristotle reminded us. Logic and common sense begin with our rational, sensory, and intuitive senses and how they appropriately and rightly direct us. We have a feeling about being people that want to make sense of things, and that gives us personal confidence and pride in who we are. We believe we are reasonable creatures and not an unreasonable something. We believe we need to feel this way, because when we don't we fall into depression and self-hate. Irrational thinking can depress us. When we return to thinking like the valuable person we are, we feel truly human again.

A personal feeling of rational worth is very important to us. We cannot rise above our thoughts. We use the parameters of logic to guide our sense of worth as persons. We feed off the praise and love of others and the recognition we get as people of common sense, all of which confirms our worth as reasonable and rational persons. We feel like persons of worth when we know our thinking is straight and not crooked.

Why is it that the evidence — from our own experience as rational, logical persons and how we function best with the use of rationality and common sense — is constantly marginalized and rejected by secular thinkers as no evidence of our unique value? To the individual, it is compelling evidence of who we are as persons. A lack of logic and clear thinking should stop any reductionist belief in its tracks. But it hasn't. This shows that they do not regard either logic or personhood as important features of who we should see ourselves to be.

Reason must take into account the amazing achievements of humans.

Technology, engineering, and science, with all their related fields and achievements, are best explained as the results of a person, not an animal or a machine. The accomplishments of humans are mental feats, sparked by the unlimited imagination of the human mind. Just think of a jet fighter that can fly at super impressive speeds and master unthought-of maneuvers, while transmitting and receiving data in split second timing, and so much more! This is nothing less than a 21st-century marvel. Drones, space endeavors, the internet, astounding medical achievements, and amazing weapons of warfare should convince anyone that the human is almost a candidate for being an object of worship. Many more marvels are in the works, too.

Where did all this unbelievable achievement come from? Did it come from a drop of lifeless, unintelligent, primordial soup? (And where did the soup come from?) And if we did come for the primordial soup, does that answer lift your spirit to feeling a sense of real value, without which none of us can function with pride? Does it confirm your sense of right thinking? Or does the belief that you are a person made in the image of God make more sense of these amazing achievements? That's an image that makes sense as an adequate explanation of our origin. Which sounds more likely and convincing to you? Which is the better use of logic?

Consider also, that the great achievements we have cited have all been made as the result of knowledge that has compounded with each generation. And the knowledge we now possess is due to all who have advanced the understanding of our world over the small span of known human history. From then to the present, no indication of evolutionary progress has been observed in the development of the human creature. This questions the validity of any claims of these advances being evidence of evolutionary progress, either mental or physical. It is inconceivable that we have no trace of an increase in human development that has enabled the human creature to make such huge strides in such a short time. The possession of logical mental processes indicate who we are by nature and are evident in the these achievements as proof enough to convince us that we are a species of a different order. Besides, where in the definition of natural selection is the ability to provide for use of imagination and reason (which is innate in all of us) to reach such heights. It's insistence on an unintelligent process as our origin does not come near to an adequate source for the amazing rationality and powers of our imagination.

Creative mental strength validates our personhood and worth.
By standing in awe of what our creative mental strengths can imagine and our minds actualize, we validate our personhood and our worth.

The mind/brain of a human is the most complicated organ we know. It is powered by passion, imagination, sensitivity, skepticism, ingenuity, the development of tactical skills, unbelievable focus and mental force, plus logistical and strategic planning that directs all of its achievements. On the emotionally warm side are our human strengths: life, empathy, love, kindness, trust, commitment, honor, personal sacrifice for the good of others, humanitarian urges, and well, more than we can catalogue of good emotions that can achieve, encourage, and build heavenly relationships. The ugly side is, unfortunately, equally impressive in a decayed and degrading way.

Because some see the mind of man as a source for only goodness and great achievements, we should not forget the unbelievable horror all of our human abilities can produce when their motivation is nakedly evil. The evidence suggests a profound fear of humans on the one hand and on the other, respect for the almost unlimited potential of human abilities for goodness. All — both the good and the evil — use of our free will possesses potential for what is totally destructive or astoundingly constructive. It is the gift of free will and our resultant choices that make the difference. Ethical values are by far the most important factor in the understanding and betterment of human behavior.

An unbiased reading of the first three chapters of the book of Genesis in the Bible has given rise in the minds of many to the acknowledgement of its accuracy in depicting the human condition. From 1:27 to 3:24 and beyond in the rest of the Bible, we travel the road of goodness and greatness that can, with bad choices, sink into the very pit of evil and its consequences. No more accurate description of human history has been written. The road has repeated itself to the present day.

Conscious Awareness of Complexity
Somewhere, and not even hidden to our consciousness, is this awareness of our being so much more than just a product of trillions of random happenings over billions of years.

Imagine (but don't run a test) what would happen if we turned to our spouse and said with conviction in our voice, "You appear to me to be reflecting nothing more than who you are: the product of some random unfortunate, unintelligent happening." What a lift it would give her/him! With a belief like that about ourselves, we can think only one thing: we are a sad happening — better to not be a happening at all.

But with the belief that we are made in the image of a God who loves us and has provided for us forgiveness and even grace, we can rise to the highest of our human potential and goodness. If we so choose, with moral sensitivities alive, we could create a much better society where love, goodness, and justice pave the way to true fulfillment and happiness. It feels to us that we are made for better things than we have carved out for ourselves in human history. Our choice has been, graphically put, a choice between life or death.

We always believe we can. Where did that thought come from? You now should know. To reach ever higher, not lower, in our beliefs is our true path to greatness. Our choice will always depend on what we believe.

Evidence from Spiritual Awareness
Our consciousness can also give evidence of a spiritual nature that defies our best definitions.

We know it; we feel it; and yet it has no apparent physical cause. It belongs in the mind and the human spirit and shares the same etherial qualities that make us aware of our value. By far the majority of humankind throughout human history have attributed this awareness to a higher cause and, hence, to a spiritual root. This innate awareness of the human spirit — something that could not be attributed to us by blind chance happenings over myriads of time — logically calls for reasonable explanation, not shabby dismissal. The theory of evolution and a materialistic view of who we are attempts to deny us what, by our nature, we sense we are. The logical conclusion to an atheist's belief is the futility of living. Suicides have been the result of beliefs that have led to feelings of worthlessness. It is not who we are.

What is the nature of this evidence from how humans have felt about themselves down through the ages? As you might imagine, it is claimed to be subjective and, therefore, unreliable (merely what we think and feel about ourselves). The objective facts of the matter are easily verified — hence, the value given to them. Subjective facts (no less facts because they can't be objectively verified) are demoted to less than valid evidence. Why? Are our experiences and feelings about ourselves less real than our experiences of the outside physical world? Of course not. But can we rely on them as much as we can rely on objectively verified facts? Yes, because of the universality and commonality of such feelings. Evidence can mount up to where it can no longer be disregarded and is beyond a reasonable doubt. Our experiences of ourselves are valid evidence — beyond a reasonable doubt.

If you still believe we are deceived by our feelings of worth, then you have to believe we are nothing more than hapless migrants, wading through a world of ultimate and futile agony. We would be, of all creatures, most miserable. Welcome to the true "theatre of the absurd."

Nothing gives us more value than to see our origin in God, himself, because no other source makes more sense. Amazingly, we are part of the evidence of who and what our source, by nature, must also be.

A Fulfilling Life

If we must feel worthy (and our human experience certainly points an unwavering finger to that need), nothing will affect more of our life than this quest for personal value.

If we believe we are persons, made in God's image, our life can find its greatest satisfaction in a life of justice and fairness for all, love for God and ourselves and as a result, love for all God's creatures. The life we should live is summed up in the words of Paul, writing to the Galatians, "…love, joy, peace, patience, kindness, goodness, faithfulness, gentleness, and self control." And this only because our value is grounded in a belief that acknowledges our Creator and the efficacious design he graciously gave us.

However, there is a needed provision that this life also craves: forgiveness for our failings, a new start with our slate wiped clean. Therefore, this experience that is offered to us by our God creates the hope of a fullness of life for imperfect creatures and becomes the foundation for a meaningful relationship with our source. Ask yourself, is this a great way to live, or not? Forgiveness makes no sense if we believe morals are self-made and, therefore, we are not accountable for them to others. Nor does failure or success make sense if we are robotically managed by our brains.

Who am I? I am, most certainly, a person by nature, exhibiting all the characteristics of personhood.

The Fatal Blow

We have learned that some philosophers, in an effort to dismiss all things non-material, tell us consciousness is just an illusion; it is not real. Wait! How can anyone be "conscious" of the fact that "consciousness" is not real if consciousness is just an illusion? How can you know an illusion from something that is real if you have never known the reality? Those who propose these improbable secular theories about who we are have just created a logical noose with which to hang themselves. There is no way out of their dilemma. Without honestly admitting their theory is illogically based on an incorrect and incomplete assumption, they must resort to denial, even if they sound unintelligent and even if they resort to illogical and ridiculous statements about the reality of an immaterial world and, for good measure, invalidate the experiences of all humankind? As they say in the courts of law, I rest my case.

This selective and crooked way of thinking, based only on the facts they want considered, belongs only to crooked thinkers who are looking for a way to deny consciousness and all things of the spirit. To them, logic, truth, reason, and the testimony of human experience just get in their way. Wow! Is this a desperate defense of their position, or is it what it is: unintelligent and puerile thinking?

We are told by others that our consciousness is just a feeling that won't go away. How do they know that? It's another mindless answer without evidence of any sort to support it.

If consciousness is an illusion, then so are all of these feelings: love, happiness, fulfillment, value, purpose, fear, hate and all the thoughts of our mental world. All are also not verifiable or real. They are supposed to lose their reality simply because some intellectual, in an act of hubris, tells us consciousness — and therefore, all that stems from it — is an illusion. This kind of thinking destroys our faith in human intelligence. It ends up with everything being an illusion, even our existence. Then pinch yourself before this thinking leads you into insanity. Maybe the pain will bring you to your senses. How have we managed to achieve all that humans have achieved if we lack the important element of personhood and self-consciousness? We humans, by our experience of ourselves, define self-consciousness. No one can live and act for one day as if self-consciousness is not a reality.

The proponents of the illusionary nature of consciousness also actually admit they do not know how consciousness could have evolved by natural selection — another admission with which they turn the gun back at themselves. We have just stumbled on a gaping hole in the theory of natural selection. Perhaps it is just in our genes, they surmise. Somehow, they seem to be very eager to get rid of all that stands opposed to their sacred cow: a false belief in a naturalistic, materialistic origin that has not so much as a smidgin of solid evidence.

Please don't get caught in this kind of thinking. Don't sell your faith out to speculations. Give due regard to the experiential facts of your own human sensibilities. There is nothing unintelligent about believing universal human experiences and the trust in them they call for. Consider the alternative. To deny our own senses and tell us to live with a belief that no one can live with is certainly an irrational "faith." Philosophical insanity is what it should be called.

Takeaway Points

• I am a person, and that's not all that has to be said. Being a person in the likeness of the greatest person that exists, our Creator, is the start of an amazingly healthy self-image.

• Accept nothing less than the feeling of importance that being a unique and wonderful person gives you.

• Knowing you are a person is also knowing your source, who gave you life, must also have been a person and/or greater.

• The ultimate cause of humans (an intelligent, personal being we call God) imparts his own sense of worth to the creatures made in his image. Think again of how valuable you must be.

• Respect all other persons. They have been made in the same image as you.

• There is no greater sense of worth than one that starts with the belief that you have been made in the image of God.

• Remember the characteristics intrinsic to being a person and cherish them:

  - A person is a living being, an individual unit, who possesses the gift of life.
  - We are creatures who think and possess a mind capable of rationality and creativity, abstract thought, and planning, etc.
  - We are creatures that feel and have complex emotions.

- We are creatures that possess a moral sense of what is good and evil.
- We are creatures that can choose our own way in life and decide our own actions. We possess a free will to make our own choices.
- We are self-conscious beings, consciously apprehending our existence.
- Who are we? We are beings of a different order.

Teaching Tools

- Always lift your own and your child's self-image, and never crush it! Always, when talking to them about their worth and value, remind them of who gives them worth and why.

- When they are down on themselves, remind them of how damaging that is and how they need to remember again who gives them the greatest reason to value themselves. It's a good thing to not insult their Creator God.

- When depressed, double your efforts at lifting their self-image.

- Show them how animals can think, but they can do so only in a limited, reactionary way. Then show them how humans can think and what their thinking has accomplished.

- Point out how they can think so much more amazingly than their pet. Pets do not communicate with language like they can.

- Talk of the difference between the thinking required to react meaningfully to what happens and abstract thinking that plans things not yet thought of.

- When they can comprehend these issues, discuss how water does not rise above its own level. A human does not give birth to a creature that is more advanced in its nature than itself. Show, in nature, that nature does not create a living thing of a superior order to itself. It can make small adaptations, but never a new and better order. A tree may vary its shape and features to meet the demands of a prevailing wind. A fish cannot give birth to a dog. Only someone greater than we are can design and create us. It's the reason why, in nature, we don't see one creature design and create another that is more intelligent than itself.

- Be the teacher of the fact that inanimate things cannot create something that is animate.

- Explain how we can respond emotionally and intelligently to people, things, and events, etc. Animals can, too, but to a much smaller degree. We can consider the consequences of our emotions, both immediate and reaching to decades ahead; animals can't. However, we can change our emotions at will in opposition to the promptings of circumstances; animals can't.

- Make your child aware of the moral decisions we make between good and evil that affect ourselves and others and the nation as a whole. The nature of an animal's moral sensitivity is of a lesser order. We are creatures of a different and higher order. Value is gained by making good moral decisions. For instance, lying devalues us; truth increases our value.

- We have free choice to do whatever we choose to do, and can do so in the opposite way from what our circumstances may suggest. It's not just a matter of having greater freedom of choice than an animal, but of a human choice that gives evidence that we are of a different order of life. It is choosing intelligently and personally, not because we are robots controlled by the physical matter that comprises our brain.

- Our sense of ourselves is so different. We can criticize ourselves, value, stand outside of ourselves, and drive ourselves to do what we don't want to do for some abstract value that we treasure. Understand your self, and you will understand a creature unlike any other.

- Separate who we are from what we do. Highly value your child for who they are, but redirect errant behavior.

6 — Around the World — Other Belief Systems

(In this chapter the word "God" will be capitalized when he is seen to be a person and will be in lower case when he is not regarded to be a person. However, the pronouns used of god will have no meaning, as is the understood case in Hinduism, for example, and therefore, they can be capitalized or lower case).

Materialism, Evolution, and Postmodernism are not the only dominant influences on the way people in the Western World think about themselves today. So, let's take a quick survey of how some non-Judeo-Christian religions have affected the way Westerner's think about their world and themselves (Who am I?). We are trying to build a firm foundation for a healthy self-worth by finding good reasons beside just our good behavior to think highly of ourselves, because behavior and personal performance change the way we think of ourselves from one moment to the next.

Who we are is going to be defined for each of us individually, because both our beliefs and our personal performance determine how we are thinking about ourselves in the moment. The question is, will we find a firm foundation in other belief systems or religions to think highly of ourselves, or only in the Judeo-Christian beliefs that have been dominant in the Western world?

So far we have reasoned from:

- The evidence of who we know ourselves to be as creatures of a different order — persons.

- The clear evidence of design we see from bio-chemistry's discoveries — especially cellular research — and from our functioning.

- The knowledge that we are living creatures and our understanding of life is more than what biology alone can tell us. Life also contains non physical elements, one being what we have simply called the "information in our software."

- The facts from how we instinctively experience ourselves, facts that are obvious and real to us all every day.

Life gives to each of us a uniqueness that can be observed in the variations of inanimate nature. Human life, however, is understandably of a higher order and an advancement on that of other animals and is even more diverse in the way it is manifested physically, emotionally, and in our temperament and personality.

As we begin the study of other religious beliefs, we need to keep uppermost in our minds the facts we have experienced about ourselves that give us significance and uniqueness among other creatures. We are persons with the ability to think, plan, and design abstractly. We weigh detailed evidence and reason logically with purpose. We are beings with complex emotional systems that we use all day long in ways still beyond our full understanding of how they fully function. Both our rational and emotional systems are capable of making decisions, creating, designing, and constructing ingenious equipment and technological marvels. We are complicated social creatures and cooperate with each other to perform the teamwork required for detailed logistical operations and meaningful relationships. We are self-conscious beings like no other. We are moral creatures who value truth and love and know the difference between good and evil. Do other beliefs give us this sense of worth? Better or worse?

We should also be aware of the well established craze in Western societies to incorporate Eastern thought and behavior into our beliefs and lives. This is being done without much thought and without noticing the contradictions and clashes Eastern beliefs have with our own. Contradiction confuses and dilutes our other beliefs. Also, most people never stop to examine the effect their thoughts and actions have on themselves and their self-worth. Beliefs that contradict each other can result in our mind introducing crooked thinking. And remember, we are what we think! But as we shall see, some of these Eastern beliefs also devalue our self-worth.

The loss of solid reasons that form a convincing foundation for our value as human beings is damaging to people who struggle with depression and anxiety. Those who want a belief about themselves that will lift their performance and stand the test of straight and rational thinking will find themselves deprived. Unfortunately, when something is unreasonable, it can become reasonable and hence, believable to us if we make it a part of how we live. Self-worth is all about what we firmly believe and act on. Therefore, it quickly becomes who we are.

The beliefs of the countless religions and sects worldwide are too numerous to consider here, nor do many of them provide important additions to the major beliefs I will introduce to you. Buddhism, Hinduism, and Zen Buddhism have been introduced to the West mainly via the New Age movement and the ubiquitous practice and teachings of yoga. The visits of the Dalai Lama have influenced many who research in the area of neuroscience. Because we are one human race, it should be important to understand the way people around the world view themselves.

Hinduism

This is one of the religions that has had a profound influence on Western culture, especially in the past 50 years or so, and the West has changed as a result. Its influences are strongest in India, the second most populous country in the world and the world's largest democracy.

Hinduism, unlike most religions, is an enigmatic, contradictory, complicated, conglomerate of beliefs. In the terms westerner's use, it can be called any and all of the following: polytheistic, pantheistic, monotheistic, agnostic, and even atheistic. Odd that it can be defined as agnostic and atheistic, but so malleable are its beliefs that this is not surprising. To add to the impossibility of summing up such diversity, it is constantly changing its beliefs as they are being added to and redefined by its numerous sects.

The following fundamental beliefs are taken from its vast sacred scriptures[24], of which the most famous is the Bhagavad Gita. Contradictions in beliefs and non-reasonable statements are regarded as mysterious and, therefore, not contradictory or illogical in nature to the Hindu. So expect contradictions. This neatly, of course, removes the charge of

---

[24] Hinduism's sacred writings, written from about 1400 BC to 500 AD, form copious volumes of various instructions, stories, hymns, and rituals. Their sacred literature is comprised of: *The Vedas* (the oldest writings, which includes hymns, ritual and prayers); *The Upanishads* (secret teachings in the form of treatise); *Ramayana and Mahabharata* (epic tales); *Bhagavad Gita* (the most sacred book and most widely read, it is a short story of salvation via moral and social behavior and devotion above self to one of the gods); *The Puranas* (legends of the gods, demons, and ancestors, describing rituals).

inconsistency. These contradictions are seen in Hinduism to contain wisdom and, also, to remind us that our minds cannot understand Brahman, the Hindu's god of sorts. Therefore, we are exhorted to not react negatively to what are apparent contradictions. Christians also talk of mystery, but draw a sharp distinction between what contradicts logic and reason and what is simply mysterious because it is beyond our understanding due to our limited knowledge.

Teachings

Before Hinduism answers our question "Who am I?" here are some of its teachings that will give you a general idea of its complexity and how that question may be answered.

- *Brahman,* the eternal one, is a three-in-one god, but not in the same sense or meaning as the triune Christian God. Brahma is the creator, Vishnu is the preserver, and Shiva, the destroyer. Together, they are called the Hindu Triad. All the sects believe in Brahman, the three-in-one god. Beyond just the number three, there is no resemblance to the Christian Triune God: Father, Son, and Holy Spirit, one God in three persons,

- The Hindu three-in-one god has multiplied until there are millions of them, now!

- *The Castes* that form the caste system also multiplied from the original four into a very large number.

- *Reincarnation* is the rebirth of each soul, which through virtuous living at each rebirth, can rise to a higher state.

- That "higher state" is *nirvana,* the release of the soul from its almost endless rebirths into becoming nothing more than a part of Brahman or the universe, losing its sense of individuality.

• *Submission to Fate:* Man is not separate from Brahman (the multiplied three-in-one god) but part of Brahman. Therefore, submission to fate and inevitability is the discipline that forms the essence of a successful life and is seen as guiding us through whatever we must face of life's experiences. Fate is a nebulous, passive acceptance of what is and whatever will happen. Fate is, therefore, seen as something everyone can accept and believe in.

• *The Law of Karma,* the belief that good always comes from good and evil, from evil. We often hear talk about good or bad karma.

• Dharma, the laws of the moral order. Each individual must follow these laws to reach nirvana.

• *Yogas,* disciplines that enable the individual to control and manage the body and their emotions, and also to follow Dharma, the moral law. It aids in the acceptance of fate. Everyone must follow Dharma in order to reach the state of nirvana. So Hinduism, like most religions, believes in the necessity of moral law.

Hinduism is tolerant of ALL other religions, with no concern for beliefs in the various religions that contradict each other and/or Hinduism. In Postmodernism, the elevation of tolerance and sympathy for oppressed elements of society is also seen, by some of them, as the main principle of an excellent life. It also reveals that the roots of Postmodernism, at least to some degree, have their deep penetration into Hinduism's tolerance and acceptance of every belief.

In both Postmodernism and Hinduism, there is little concern for absolute truth. Tolerance, in Hinduism, is advocated as a path to wisdom and an avoidance of confusion. Hence, truth is subjugated to the demands of social harmony that Hinduism promotes with its tolerant behavior. Hindus are even proud of the fact that there have not been any violent conflicts among them. However, Hindus are not averse to going to war with their neighbors, which appears to most people to be, at the least, intolerant behavior.

A Closer Look at Brahman

To try to understand Brahman, the philosophical principle (not a personal being) behind the universe and all mankind, we need to absorb the following enigmatic beliefs. Brahman is...

- The ultimate principle that is the foundation and underlying factor for all reality.

- Brahma (the first in the three in one god) was not caused by anything, nor does he cause anything (a seeming contradiction in terms of the fact that he is named the creator). Hinduism would say that in contradiction lies a mystery that hides wisdom.

- He *appears* to be the ultimate spirit, having as the Upanishad (one of the sacred scriptures of Hinduism) states, nothing inside or outside.

- Words cannot describe him, nor can the mind reach him. The mind will only come away confused and baffled if it tries to understand him.

- Brahman is more like a philosophic principle than a person, a being, or even an active principle in the universe.

192

- Because of his mysterious and enigmatic nature, we can mediate on him but not worship or adore him. The pronoun "him" has really no meaning at all when used of Brahman.

What Does Hinduism Tell Us About Who We Are?

- Brahman is remote from humans in that he is *not concerned or interested in what is going on in the world or in human life*, and we are part of this remote, disinterested, universal spirit. That should give us a big hint as to who we are in Hindu thinking.

- Because Brahman is not a person, we cannot attribute our personhood to Brahman. Therefore, any sense of worth that being a person gives us must come from other beliefs. (It should be noted that sources other than a person cannot give any worth to personhood). There is a constant tension in Hinduism between being a creature of inherent worth because we are part of Brahman and loosing our individual identity in being one with Brahman, which is the goal of all Hinduism's sacred practices.

- Although Brahman is the creator, we can have no personal relationship with him. Nor does he reach out to us to engage with us or even care about us.

- We are part of Brahman's spirit and he is the spirit of the universe so, in this sense, we also are part of his divine essence that is the universe. Remember, this essence is unfathomable and remote. We are a part of god and our lives are purposeless, directed only by fate. It is fate, not purpose, that we must focus on in life.

- We can also be seen as real since Brahman is the ultimate reality, and we are also the truth in an undefined way. This is us!

- We are not only material beings with bodies, we have an "atman," which is the self or soul. This soul is what is released in the state of nirvana.

- We are not individuals, although we appear on earth in bodily form to be individuals. Apart from our behavior, we have no foundation for an individual sense of worth.

All of this does not add up to being individuals of importance. A foundation for self-worth is missing. It should also be apparent that we have lost a reason to believe in almost all we treasure most about ourselves: our self-consciousness and personhood, and all that we find satisfying as individual creatures.

The reason behind this loss of a real basis for individual worth is simple to understand. All Hinduism is based on the belief that the universe is divine (read, god) and the divine is the universe. We are finally part of it and, in some way, finally absorbed into the universe.

Therefore, we are god, but in a very impersonal, remote, untouchable way — an impersonal universal existence that you are simply a part of. An impersonal being doesn't think, feel, or decide to act, and it does not care one bit about other individuals. The universe is absorbed in Brahman, who is the spirit of the universe. All material elements of the universe also do not care — a rock doesn't, the ocean doesn't, the forces of nature don't. Think how the impersonal nature of Brahman and his being all things leaves us with no distinct personal value. It supports their need to believe in fate, which also removes most of the incentive to be someone or achieve. We must find other motivations to achieve.

Being a part of Brahman and the universe is one of the beliefs in Hinduism that has changed the way many Western people now talk about their relationship to the universe. They put their wishes out there for the universe to respond to, and some even pray to the dumb, inanimate forces of a disinterested universe. It sounds so much like a return to the idolatry of the nations in ancient biblical days. The universe is being treated as a substitute for a personal, loving God. But the ultimate reality — all reality for Hinduism — is of an uncaring, disinterested, remote spirit, and we are also a part of this disinterested reality.

The Bhagavad Gita, in a famous passage, defines Brahman (god) and us (because we are part of Brahman). In the passage, the father is talking to his son, who wants to know what reality, and Brahman is…

> "Place this salt in water and come to me tomorrow morning." "
> "I cannot see the salt. I only see water," *(says Svetaketu, the son)*.
> Svetaketu did as he was commanded and in the morning, his father said to him, "Bring me the salt you put into the water last night."
> Svetaketu looked into the water, but could not find it, for it had dissolved.
> His father then said: "Taste the water from this side. How is it?"
> "It is salt."
> "Taste it from the middle. How is it?"
> "It is salt."
> "Taste it from that side. How is it?"

"It is salt."

"Look for the salt again, and come again to me."

The son did so, saying: "I cannot see the salt. I only see water."

His father then said: "In the same way, O my son, you cannot see the spirit.

But in truth he is there. An invisible and subtle essence is the Spirit of the whole universe. That is Reality. That is Truth. THOU ART THAT!"

So, the Bhagavad Gita makes it clear: Brahman is the spirit of the universe, and we are that, too. We are not individuals, except that our bodies give that impression. Hinduism believes selfhood is an illusion. The universe is reality — an inanimate, uncaring, disinterested, and remote reality. We are nothing more than these things. We might ask, does that explain mind, self-consciousness, intelligence? If we are spirit, which is equated with the inanimate universe and with Brahman, do we have no individual existence? Correct! Then, of what value are we? Apparently, no personal, individual value at all. We must simply follow fate, which is our guide to attain a successful life.

Add to this, I will have to progress through many reincarnations from the lowest of life's organisms to the highest. Then, if I exhibit a noble display of virtue and principle, plus obedience to the rituals and rights of Hinduism, finally, I will enter nirvana, in which I have no self existence or consciousness, only to be a part of the whole, which is Brahman. "Why live?" is our response to all this. Hope is gone, along with self-worth, and I end up with no meaning and no reasonable foundation for believing in myself or my worth.

This makes the Western craze of throwing our wishes out into an inanimate universe seem rather uneducated and, frankly, dumb. What can we expect as a response? The same as you can expect from worshipping an idol of stone: nothing, except whatever fate brings.

To talk of putting our wishes, wants, or needs out into the universe, as though the immaterial, impersonal universe can hear, cares, or can respond to any of our wishes is very unreal — in fact, unintelligent. The universe has no qualities that personhood requires to be able to communicate or react to a person and their wants and needs. This language, which is commonplace among Westerners now, is rooted in these Hindu beliefs about reality, god, and who we are. Let's evaluate what we are believing with a little more sanity than this.

Buddhism

Buddhism has also made an impact on Western thought and life. No understanding of Eastern religions would be complete without a study of Buddhism. It has made inroads into China and Japan, as well as Tibet and India. In subtle ways, it has made its mark on Western philosophies. You will often hear people reflecting the teachings of Buddha in their conversations and using phrases that mirror its thinking, too.

Therefore, we need to understand what is helpful, and what is not, in the thinking and behavior of Buddhism.

History
Buddha (Siddhartha Gautama) was apparently strongly influenced by the Hindu sacred writings called the Upanishads. In Buddhism, there are many reflections of the teachings of Hinduism that can be directly traced to Hindu origins, alongside a rejection of the caste system.

Buddhism began in India around 500 BC. It is very different in many ways from Hinduism. For example, it denies the authority of the Vedas (part of the Hindu sacred scriptures) with their hymns, rituals, prayers, and secret teachings.

Siddhartha Gautama was the founder of Buddhism, and many fictional stories are told of his life. He became known as the Buddha. The Buddha, which means "The Enlightened One," received his enlightenment while sitting for seven days under a fig tree, where with the help of intense meditation, he supposedly reached the enlightened state of nirvana. He was then no longer known by his given name, but was called The Buddha, the enlightened one.

Beliefs and Practices

Here is a brief summary of the main beliefs to give you an idea of what Buddhism teaches.

Luxury and self-torture are to be disdained if the path to enlightenment, knowledge, and insight, along with calm and a higher knowledge, are to be found and nirvana experienced.

This path consists of accepting the Three Noble Truths and the Eightfold Path, which is the fourth Noble Truth.

The Four Noble Truths Are:

1. The existence of suffering.

2. The cause of suffering is our desires and our thirst for happiness and prosperity.

3. The end of all suffering is found in the giving up all cravings, passion, and desire.

4. The acceptance of the eight-fold path is the essential practice for all Buddhists.

The Eightfold Path Is:

1. Having the right views — accepting the Four Noble Truths and the Eightfold Path.

2. The right resolve — renouncing all sensual pleasure, having no ill will toward anybody, and causing no harm to any living creature.

3. Right speech — don't lie, slander, abuse anyone, or indulge in idle talk.

4. Right behavior — don't kill any living creature; only take what is given to you, and do not engage in unlawful sexual acts.

5. Right occupation — earn your living in a way that harms no one.

6. Right effort — strive to prevent any evil qualities from arising in you, and abandon any evil qualities. Strive for good qualities and encourage those you do possess to grow, increase, and be perfected.

7. Right contemplation — be observant, strenuous, alert, contemplative, and free of desire and sorrow.

8. Right meditation — enter and experience the four degrees of meditation, which concentration produces.

Therefore, Buddhism accepts the need of moral law to guide a human life.

Does Buddhism Worship a God?

Some say yes, and some say no. The reason for this ambiguity is that Buddhism has venerated[25] The Buddha who, sometime after his death, was deified (became the equivalent to god) by some of his followers. However, Buddhism denies the existence of a personal God. So, it is nearest to the truth to say Buddhism is not a religion with a god.

───────────────

[25] *Chinese Buddhist Verse*, Richard Robinson trans., Greenwood Publication, 1954, page 48.

No Intelligent Source for Humans — Very Sad News

This robs humans of an origin that springs from an intelligent, personal source. The individual has no intrinsic value or worth. Man is seen as worthless because he has only a fleeting existence. His body is also a hindrance to him, not the glorious creation of an intelligent personal God. He must struggle and fight against his desires for, as the Buddha has said, the essence of Buddhism is to:

> Cease from all sin,
> Get virtue,
> And purify the heart.

With this view of man, Buddhism, therefore, cannot explain the amazing detail of the universe that physics has revealed to us, or the unbelievable intelligent design of a human being's intricate physical system, let alone his immaterial makeup or the origin of his intelligence[26]. The existence of evidence that points to intelligence, purpose, and a designer has no explanation, is not addressed, and is simply ignored.

Buddhist beliefs have, therefore, become an Eastern advocacy for a secular understanding of our universe, for biological evolution, and for the work of a materialistic science in general. This has made Buddhism popular among some psychiatrists and neuroscientists who want to find a way to include a religion of sorts in their lives, but exclude all belief in a personal God[27].

---

[26] See Ray W. Lincoln, *Compelling Evidence for God*.

[27] One such "convert" is Howard C. Cutler, M.D who authors the Dalai Lama's concepts for living as a true Buddhist and finding happiness in *The Art of Happiness.*

The final goal for all Buddhists is nirvana. The word means "to be extinguished". In a state of being extinguished (nirvana), desire together with suffering are also extinguished.[28] The Buddhist attempt to define the divine has used words, like nothingness and the void, which feels like an attempt to synchronize their concepts of god and nirvana, both of which are nothingness.

We are asked to accept this dismal, depressing reduction of Judeo-Christian beliefs about both the explanation for and purpose of the universe as a mechanistic model. Humans then have an inanimate origin and are stripped of intrinsic worth, struggling against all passions and desires to find meaning only in obedience to the tenets of Buddhism. Take a breath and conjure a happy thought to keep you from feeling rather sad!

A Dismal Pantheism
All pantheists (and that includes all Eastern religions) lower our value so that we, too, must hope to be incorporated into some incomprehensible divine essence and/or be absorbed into nature, losing what we have treasured most: our individuality, uniqueness, and self-worth. To lose all self-worth (and self-worth is doubtfully real to these religions) in the final step of our existence into nirvana means we amount to nothing in the long run, and there is no intrinsic value to humanity to be lost. Try living without desire or self-worth and see what it does to the noble quest of being everything you can be.

---

[28] For a more comprehensive survey of Buddhism and its beliefs, see any reliable summary of the world's religions, or for a Christian perspective, a survey is found in *The Handbook of Today's Religions,* by Josh McDowell and Don Stewart.

Motivation and Meaning, Limited or Lost

Western societies, being founded on Christian beliefs, have made the dream and advancement of human achievement possible. In both Hinduism and Buddhism, there is no basis for the motivation we need to achieve and to strive for a sense of fulfillment that makes all ingenious achievements possible — no motivation to lift us off the ground and begin our flight to personal greatness. I have already shown that solid evidence and sound logical conclusions from science and reason show we are much more than this devalued view of ourselves. Our beliefs about ourselves are very, very important if we want to reach for the stars and be more than just nature — rather, be truly human nature. Only then can we know what it means to be a creature made in God's image.

There are good things in what every belief system around the globe seeks to accomplish. But some distinct differences in the results of each system of beliefs are clearly visible in the way of life we can observe in different areas of the world. Some areas are hot beds for ingenuity and creativeness, and some are not. When humans see themselves as nothing more than a part of the natural world, nothing more than the rock on the mountain or the sand of the seashore or the water of the ocean, they lose something vital to the pulse of life that beats longingly in their human minds.

As Li Po's poem entitled *The Birds Have Vanished Into the Sky*[29] tells us, the mountain (or for that matter, the seashore or the ocean), in the final analysis, is you. All inanimate things that are of less value than the miracle of an intelligent, purpose-driven human life, are us and, depressingly, also our future. We came from lifeless matter, these beliefs tell us, and

------

[29] See Ivan Granger's, *Li Po — The Birds Have Vanished Into the Sky*.

will return to it, forgotten, having lived meaninglessly. Why go through the suffering of life if that is all there is to it. The "real you," in Buddhism, is nothing but nature in the form of matter, devoid of personhood, personality, and self-worth, which Buddhism in its essence dismisses from our minds and dreams. These dreams (desires), we are told, we should not have entertained in the first place. Eastern meditation, we are told, will carry us to this valueless realization. Your selfhood and personhood are nothing but a disappointing illusion — in fact, for Buddhism, a shabby sin of sorts.

As a result, Buddhists seek to avoid pain and the cry of personal desires in order to be great. In the process, they woefully lower their horizon of life, changing possibilities to a pathetic hope, in the end, of nothingness. Don't settle for a belief that fails to address the personal dimensions of who we are.

Jesus, referring to the miracles he did, motivates us with these words: "Greater things than these will you do." This makes us feel unlimited and conscious of our ability to do great things. The best for us all is still to be, as far as Jesus is concerned. We need a faith that can support, both intellectually and emotionally, our sense of personal worth and preserve all of our passions that make us reach metaphorically for those lights high in the sky.

Zen Buddhism

The Origin of Zen Buddhism

Buddhism has many sects with variations of practice and belief. Theravada Buddhism was largely the Buddhism of India until the invasion by Islam in the 13th century AD. In other countries (mainly China and Japan) another form is practiced: Mahayana Buddhism, which is more liberal and relevant to modern life. Zen Buddhism began about a millennium after the death of Buddha.

If there are different demands for the moral paths and practices we must tread to arrive in nirvana, how can any of these sects of Buddhism be the only way to nirvana?

The Focus and Essence of Zen

In the West, Zen Buddhism (a branch of Mahayana Buddhism) is widely known. It focuses on meditation and prescribes the zazen (the sitting position for meditation). Cross legged and sitting on a small round cushion, the practitioner takes up the zazen position (described in great detail) and meditates with chants interspersed. This is done daily and at prescribed times for the devoted.

No Written Scriptures or Sacred Writings

Zen Buddhists have no scriptures, and its tenets are transmitted from one mind to another. Its founder, Bodhidharma, explained it this way: "It is a special tradition outside the sacred writings or scriptures of Buddhism. It has no dependence on words, points directly at man, and sees into our own nature, attaining wisdom for the practitioner." As a result, the path to wisdom and to nirvana is mainly subjective in nature.

A Sisyphean Ethical Struggle

Man must extricate himself from the quicksand of his own passions. Help is from within. Frequently quoted are the words of Buddha, "Look within. You are the Buddha." So, left without any power but our own, they (like us) feel the frustration of Paul's words of despair when he tells of human experience that must go it alone: "I do not know what I am doing. For what I want to do, I do not do, but what I hate, I do[30]."

If we are left without help and a Savior, life is nothing but a Sisyphean laborious, futile effort. You may remember, the punishment the Greek gods metered out to Sisyphus for his misdeeds. He was to push a huge boulder up a hill, only to have it slip from his grasp when he reached the top and roll to the bottom, making him have to repeat the performance endlessly. All Sisyphean efforts are laborious, painful, and futile, and they develop a growing sense of failure. The human, who is made in the image of God, longs to reach out to God and get the help and forgiveness he needs to extricate himself from life's failures and find his feet again.

All this reminds me of the image of trying to extricate oneself from quicksand by pulling up strenuously on your boot laces.

No God or Creator

Also, in the true fashion of Buddhism, it denies the existence of a personal God or Creator. The world, it believes, operates

---

[30] Romans 7:15.

on the power and laws of nature (Materialism). All the factual evidence of intelligence, purpose, and design that science has uncovered in the macro and micro zones of our universe and that we can see for ourselves in our universe, calls this Buddhist belief a pathetically inadequate explanation.

Concepts for How to Live
Buddhism is made of concepts about life and how life is to be lived. All these concepts are the product of fallible, limited human reasoning. There is no measure or standard but the human's own perceptions to arrive at the truth, which Zen is certain it has discovered. Man is transitory and, therefore, like science and any system of human discovery, proceeds one funeral after another. That is all Zen Buddhism has for us. When will the next human "insightful concept" supplant this one? Add to that the belief that our body is a hindrance to living the enlightened life, and we are left to admire the Buddhist's determination and perseverance, but not their practical wisdom.

Final Thoughts
Speaking of Buddhism in all of its variations: Perhaps more damaging than some of the other Eastern religions, the human is reduced to despise his own desires and is further reduced to being a problem to himself. All humans know, at times, that they are a problem to themselves. But if this is all we are to be focused on, we are of all men most miserable.

How can such a belief lead to wisdom? Buddhists believe it can. But this and the other beliefs of Buddhism make life a matter of rigidly following a path of human struggle with little hope for the undisciplined. Those with more developed focus and determination may succeed to a point, but what is that in the grand scheme of a happy life? Don't be deceived by the beliefs of Buddhism or Zen Buddhism. According to their beliefs, we amount to nothing in the long run.

Thoughts that Linger About Reductionism

A final word about this devaluing of humans. It's not only these religions that have beliefs that devalue humans. Darwin advocated the same principles, and I paraphrase these religions and Darwinism: If we are to refuse the obvious evidence of who we are (that is, we came from a source greater than ourselves, who gave us our true worth, and that we show undeniable evidence of intelligent, purpose-driven design), we must devalue ourselves so that the source becomes something other than a person. Why?

To deny our sense of worth and bury it in our changing achievements, we will have to have come from a source that is not personal, a some*thing* not a some*one*. That's exactly what Darwin did for the generations that have followed him. He made us the product of natural forces that have no intelligence or personhood. He sent us off on the same fruitless chase for meaning that the Eastern religions fatefully resign us to. Even Darwin did not live as though his teachings were true. Trying to live that way produces humans with little ambition or desire to be the best they can be and who must lose their sense of personal grandeur and freedom. Their only escape is to act contrary to what they say they believe.

I have always been dumbfounded that an educated person wants to deny that we have a free will (the ability to make our own decisions) and wants us to believe that all our choices are the result of brain chemistry that we do not control. Surely, they experience the marvel of being free beings with freedom to choose for themselves. Then why try to argue we are in no fundamental way beings of free choice? Why do they want us to believe we are hapless robots?

I conclude that the reason is because the admission (that we operate like beings with personal freedom to choose) means we will have to look for an explanation for our origin that declares we came from a source that, at the very least, has the same innate and intelligent abilities. That's too close to our source being God!

This attempt to explain away our ability to make free choices makes no sense. And in the very attempt to do so, it proves we have the freedom to do the very thing we are denying to ourselves.

Imagine having to say:

- I looked into my wardrobe this morning and my brain chose for me what I am wearing. (Really?)

- I made for breakfast what my brain chose for me to eat. We then are not talking in the clear terms of the reality we experience.

- Watch out for this one and don't use it: The one I love and married was not my personal choice. (That will fly like a lead balloon). Tell your wife you sincerely believe that, and be prepared to spend the night in the dog house.

Why believe about ourselves what we cannot and do not experience? Why deny the evidence of all human experience — of all humans, through all the ages? The best of luck trying to live that way! You won't, without a harsh clash with reality. A religion that is reductionist (reduces our value to something less than what we experience) is not elevating or factually true to reality, either.

Confucianism

The major schools of thought in Chinese history are Confucianism (a system of ethical beliefs) and two religions (if they can be called religions): Buddhism and Taoism. All three still exert their influence in the communistic regime of China. Christianity has made great inroads and is the faith of millions of Chinese. It is technically recognized. But in reality, it is persecuted and Christians have been forced to worship and practice prayer, etc, in secret.

Confucius, born around 550 BC, the youngest of 11 children, died in his early 70's in 479 BC. Placing him in historical perspective, Buddha and Confucius were contemporaries. Socrates, Plato, and Aristotle also lived at about the same time. So, while other movements were gaining impetus in other parts of the world, Confucianism was coming to the rescue in a divided and violent China.

His youth was that of a normal boy: hunting and fishing. But at the early age of 15, he devoted himself to learning. Confucius became an itinerant teacher and established himself as the most significant influence on his country's ethical beliefs and practices. His emphasis on the veneration of one's ancestors has been rewarded by the veneration accorded him from his day to the present. Three of the most significant venerations are:

- He was honored with the full rank of Emperor in 1068 — 1086 AD, even though he was not an emperor.

- On December 31,1906 AD, by an imperial decree, he was anointed with the rank of Co-assessor with the deities, Heaven and Earth. An astounding tribute!

- Animal sacrifices were offered to him, and this obvious worship of him was recognized publicly again in 1914 by the first president of the Republic of China.

No wonder the Chinese people still revere him and read his writings and those of his disciples in the Analects[31].

To the Chinese, the phrase "Confucius says…" is equivalent to the phrases used by Christians: "Jesus said…," or "The Bible says…."

Focus on Man

The focus for our examination of the truth in other religions and quasi religions about "Who am I?" is now focused on this man and his teachings about family, society, and the peaceful functioning of the country. In other words, we will focus on one man's teachings and the changes they brought to Chinese thinking and behavior. However, God or any deity are conspicuous by their absence. Confucianism is not a religion.

The existence of the spirits of the ancestors after death and their veneration plays a central role in the thinking of Confucius and the motivations he constructs for his ethical system. This veneration amounts to worship.

---

[31] *The Analects* and three other books, *The Great Learning, The Doctrine of the Mean,* and *The Book of Mencius,* contain his teachings and were written by Confucius and his disciples.

There Is Much That Is Noble and Good About Confucianism

We see the shortcomings of Buddhism in Confucianism with one major difference: Confucianism is a much more optimistic philosophy, but still remains a form of humanism with no God or superior being to worship. Mankind is front and center. The big questions of life and the origins of all things are ignored — thus, in practice, eliminating the need for a God.

As a system of ethical beliefs, it is incomplete and deals mainly with issues that are designed to restore the already existing belief in ancestor worship and the right behavior for a country that was, at the time, steeped in wars and suffering. The complete breakdown of society and culture was threatening the Chinese people.

Confucian Doctrine

Society Must Be Saved from Destruction

The times in which Confucius lived are best understood by the word anarchy. It comes from the Greek word *anarchos* and means ruleless, or without rule or a ruler. Murderous uprisings were feared daily, and people were in a constant state of anxiety and trepidation. Mass executions were the weapon of fear used in the constant wars and surprise attacks that spared no one — male nor female, child nor adult. Soldiers were paid when they presented the heads of their victims. There are accounts of up to 400,000 being slaughtered en masse. The conquered were being thrown into boiling cauldrons, and their relatives (who were still unfortunate enough to be alive) were forced to drink the human soup[32]. The horror of being without rule and law is a lesson our world has not seriously learned after two-and-one-half millennia. Lawlessness and the oppression of power, both are the bedfellows of war and hate.

Rules and laws do not infringe on a person's freedom. They protect it. The rot that developed in the absence of morals soon decayed into the stench of these shocking, murderous sprees and vile acts that scoffed at human dignity. (Indications that this attitude has not died are still evident in China today). Any and all who were hungry for power saw the opportunity for a power grab. China was paying a horrible price for the freedom of its leaders to do whatever was right in their own eyes.

The very idea of right and wrong was being sacrificed on the altar of the leaders' desire for their own absolute human freedom. It meant that any means to achieve one's ends was the law of the day for any who aspired to power. Human rights vanished, truth was spurned, and power was enthroned. Safety and equal rights were only a dream. Society pays the cost of such lawless freedoms. When they are allowed, the powerful rule without love, tolerance, or care. Full freedom for an individual means no freedom for all, only anarchy.

These were the evil directions the nation was suffering from in the day of Confucius. He comes not as a savior, but simply a teacher — a very influential one, at that — one who infused

---

[32] Huston Smith, *The Religions of Man*, Harper and Row, 1965.

into Chinese culture some needed resistance to total decay. For this, he is to be honored.

It became the mission of his life to save the degradation of his land. Did he achieve this totally? No. But he applied the brakes to the runaway moral train[33], and the people began to taste of goodness — limited as his concept of goodness may have been. He did this with what seemed like a faith that believed in the goodness of man. If only he had found the true foundation for such an optimistic faith beyond a frustrated faith in humanity, and if only he had a solution to the failures of humans who are imperfect and in need of a saving solution. His ethical revolution, though noble and exemplary, fell short. And to this day in China, the evils of self-driven interests and the corruption of power still exist as they do worldwide.

Some of the reasons why he did not have a path that met the entire ethical needs of his society are:

- He did not understand that goodness is only found in reaching beyond ourselves to a higher power, one that is a true example of goodness.
- He failed to know that we must reach for the practice of true love (which Jesus taught) and a belief in the need for humans to be rescued from their mistakes, finding in the forgiveness of their Creator and Savior the wholeness of life that only a higher power can offer.

These shortcomings and others can be seen in the limited range of his ethical reformations and in all humanistic philosophies and religions.

---

[33] The lack of morality is a runaway train and history has repeatedly recorded humanity's slowness at learning the lesson. It is becoming again a threat in many countries.

The Principles of His Ethical Teachings

He turned first to the role the individual must play in any ethical system. That role must have the good of all as its goal. He also saw clearly that if this was to be done, the individual plays a major role in the creation of a peaceful society.

Principle One

Man must treat man with goodness and respect, and a hope of being treated the same way by others.

Hence, his most famous saying found in the Analects: "Do not impose on others what you yourself do not desire." This is the law of reciprocity. Confucius saw this as the highest virtue, while Christ taught that to love God with all our hearts... and to love our neighbor to the same degree as we love ourselves is the highest virtue.

What has become known as the Golden Rule reached its positive expression in Jesus' teaching, "Do unto others as you would have them do to you." Confucius taught the negative form of the Golden Rule. The negative aims at *doing no harm* to others and ourselves, while the positive aims at *doing good* to others and ourselves. Only in the presence of the positive is the full expression of an effective reciprocity.

Confucius almost constructed a rule that would bring peace and harmony to his society. Christ's focus was on a human finding a way of life that would bring peace, harmony, goodness, and love to all people and to ourselves. So, the

Golden Rule is a rule for the achievement of successful human relationships and is applicable to all humans.

Principle Two

The basic unit of society, for Confucius, is family. Loyalty and devotion to the family became the major motivational element in the teachings of Confucius, finding its fulfillment in ancestor veneration. Long before Confucius, the Chinese people felt the need of this focus on the family and ingrained it into their society. Confucius was restoring its importance.

Loyalty to the family meant devotion to it in order for it to become an essential factor in the healing of society. Son should honor the father and all the children should honor their elders. The responsibility that this honor brought was seen as a fixed duty of the elders to implement.

In principle, his teaching awakened a theme the Chinese people would quickly respond to. It gave him great receptivity among them. He wanted the children to cause their parents anxiety only over matters of illness, never for anything else. It was illustrated by a call to be better than the animals.

Principle Three

Confucius then saw that the model he was restoring for the home should be the model for the world beyond the home. Therefore, insightfully, he taught that the man should act as a "gentleman" to all. The definition of gentlemanly behavior was to show:

- Humility,
- Magnanimity,
- Sincerity,

- Diligence, and
- Graciousness to all.

All of this will help a person get along with those outside of the home, while being rewarded by developing a persona of honor for themselves. Noble, yes, and not without a little self reward.

But more effective than his teachings, and all-encompassing in its demand, is the need for love and truth, without which a society cannot be the peaceful, safe, harmonious world he envisaged. We surely are at our best when we love ourselves and all our neighbors. All societies fall apart into strife if truth is not established, as well as love that is the lubricant for the wheels of society. Again, Confucius' teachings, although noble, still left room for the breakdown of society.

Principle Four
A society must have structure. In the China of his day, this meant a person should act according to his stature in society: a king like a king and a father like a father, etc. So the structure is based on all leaders, from the ruler to the father, acting so as to earn respect by their appropriate behavior. Society, he believed, would change for the good if this were accomplished. Placing a sense of responsibility on the leader struck at the heart of the problem of his day: the transformation of corrupt leaders.

Principle Five
Power is exercised best by people of virtue. If control is not in the hands of the virtuous (this does not mean the perfect, because all of us are imperfect), power will corrupt people. In China, as in other nations, this principle has failed to be

executed. We humans, when left alone to police our own ethical standards, tend to fall short. Leaders have murdered their own citizens over and over again in history. David, the esteemed king of Israel, was guilty of this and of many misdeeds, but his heart was in the right place and God called him "a man after his own heart" — not a man after his own righteous standards.

So, Confucius was astute in seeing this as being the root of the problem to achieve the national wellbeing. How he escaped from paying with his life when he confronted the rulers with this, we don't know. Perhaps his gracious approach and manner was his saving factor.

Principle Six
All relationships, Confucius taught, were held together with the mutual virtue of respect. The Chinese word for this was "Li." Its meaning can be conditioned by its context, but respect seems a good English translation. Other words could be courtesy or reverence. This glue, though, does not hold all relationships firmly together. It can be a perceived behavior but does not have its roots in a heart exhibiting love, truth, and honesty. Truth and love are the only successful cements for great relationships.

Principle Seven
Acts of peace are the final element that is dominant in the teaching of Confucius. He sees them as the fruits of all that has gone before. But again, he fell short. He taught that acts of peace are things like music, poetry, and art. Such can indeed be peaceful activities, but even these can be used with spiteful or even evil intent.

These peaceful acts are necessary, but there is more that society needs to form a complete system of ethics. We find the pure acts that the ideal society should exhibit in Paul's recounting of the Fruit of the Spirit: love, joy, peace, long-suffering, kindness, goodness, faithfulness, gentleness, and self control.[34] The motivations of our hearts and its expectations and intents must be pure, first, because out of the heart emerges our behavior. The question for all acts remains: Is our heart stained with impurity or does it sparkle with purity and love for all?

Ancestor Worship Provided the Motivation

For every complete ethical system or any foundation for a successful society there must be adequate motivation. Confucius found this in the age-old Chinese practice of ancestor worship. There had to be a higher appeal and motive for changing behavior and getting results. The veneration of ancestors was restored and emphasized.

To Confucius, the veneration of ancestors included these beliefs and practices:

- Veneration of the spirits of their ancestors by the living relatives.

- Apparently, he taught that if the spirits of the dead do not receive attention, they may fail to continue their existence.

---

[34] Galatians 5:22-23

- If their needs are met, they will cause good to happen to the relatives; if not, they may cause bad things to happen. It's kind of like the way karma is supposed to work, only it was focused on the way people were to honor and worship their dead ancestors.

- Meeting their needs means, in part, supplying them with the same standard of living they enjoyed while alive.

- The ancestors may appear as ghosts to haunt the living.

- The living relatives may become afraid of the dead.

- The ancestors may actually control the fortunes of the living, so fear of reprisal is heightened.

- The ancestors may control things better than when they were alive.

- The ancestral worship may also be a way to let the dead know all is well and let them rest in peace.

- There is a strong appeal in this practice to secure the love of your family while alive and, therefore, their good treatment of you after you die.

- This all works best when the ancestors reward the living with health, children who are blessed, and prosperity.

A hazy belief in a life after death is latent in his teaching about ancestor worship.

Evaluation of Its Impact on Society Today

The teachings of Confucius have had a huge impact on the Chinese society and they still do. As the country becomes more aware of the benefits of science and technology, plus a growing envy of capitalist societies, these ethical beliefs are loosing their hold somewhat.

Confucius' teachings and his achievements are the noble work of a man on a mission, but it sadly falls short of a complete ethical system or of one that reaches the highest and noblest. It also falls short as a comprehensive understanding of our world. Only an acceptance of the highest standards of truth and love as revealed in the teachings of Jesus can truly change this world for the good.

Who Am I?

Although Confucianism holds an optimistic belief about humans, it has no message for when humans fail. It provides, as far as it goes, an admirable pattern for human behavior and belief, but it does not satisfy the yearnings of the human heart. It presents no hope for the fallen human or when self effort has become futile and empty. It offers no real foundation for a belief in our innate worth.

Islam

World Status and Growth

One more belief system (also a religion), this time in the Middle East, needs comment. Islam (the Arabic word means submission or surrender) is also known as Muslim (which means the one who submits) and has distinguished itself in a number of ways. It is the most militant of the faiths and has been so from its inception, waging war and conquering other nations.

Only 100 years after the death of Mohammad (also spelled Muhammad) its founder, it had conquered lands and created a vast empire that stretched as far as southern France and Spain to the West and eastward to include North Africa, Central Asia, and the countries all the way to the borders of China. Its advances in later history, at times also military operations, included a part of India, parts of Eastern Europe, Southeast Asia, and further into Africa. Most of its growth has been as a result of its military power and this sets it apart from other religions.

Now it has adherents in many countries around the world, including all of Europe and North America. Recently, rightwing extremists (Isis) have attempted to form a caliphate in the Middle East by military force, but they have failed. Another extremest sect of Islam, now mainly in Iran, is attempting to make an atomic bomb and threatens the world's peace. It is listed as a terrorist nation. But not all Muslims are militant. Many are peace loving and not passionate about the use of power. They claim to be only peaceful followers of Mohammed.

Islam and Christianity are the largest of the world's religions. It is hard to asses the numbers with real accuracy because, for the most part, Christianity's numbers are counted by those who *call themselves* Christians and have personally become followers of Jesus Christ, whereas Muslims are more often numbered by the residents in a country that is Islamic by rule or conquered by force. It is also the most influential religion in terms of a political force in the world today and regarded as a political threat.

We must note: The influences of Islam in the countries it has either occupied or where Muslims are present in vast numbers have also, in part, been positive. Some influences, such as the subservience of women, are obviously negative.

The Founder

It all began with Mohammed the prophet. To gain a historical perspective, he was born several thousands of years after the first writings of Judaism and Hinduism, and around one thousand years after the golden age of the Greek philosophers, the birth of Confucius, and Siddhartha Gautama (also called The Buddha), who came comparatively late to the scene of Eastern religions. Mohammed was born around 570 AD in the city of Mecca. The early deaths of both his father and mother left him to be raised by his grandfather and uncle. Unlike some of the other founders of Eastern religions in particular, he is not enveloped in mystery. A lot is known about his early days and his life as a whole.

According to evidence that surely was not fabricated, he suffered from fits early in his life. But what is most significant is that he was spiritually inclined and practiced fasting and meditation, often on his own, in the surrounding caves. He was also given to dreams. At 25, he married a wealthy 40-

year-old widow, Khadijah. It can safely be assumed he was an introvert. The existence of one true God became an early passion and this can be traced, at least in part, to his interest in Jewish and Christian Scriptures. Jewish and Christian influence was well established in Arab countries at this time and his contact with them is little in doubt.

Mohammed was poetically inclined and more of an improvisor and an extemporaneous, in-the-moment fabricator rather than a systematic thinker.[35] His writings give evidence to his style and the nature of his intelligence. His personality was somewhat retiring, of a considerate nature, kind, and showing a decisive and determined trait. He is said to have been a born leader and his sensuality, sensitivity, and emotional outbursts could result in cruel behavior that included assassinations.[36] His swings from emotions of love to hate, his vindictiveness and (on the other extreme) his gentleness were well known. His mental states of anger and peace could occur within moments of each other.[37] Was this evidence of mental imbalance, or of the hyper emotionalism of a temperament well known to us, or both? From our later investigation into how people are made at the core and how their lives are shaped, you may be able to guess his temperament. In his day, it would have been known as choleric.

At the age of 40, he had his first vision and so began the writings of the Qur'an (Koran). These visions or revelations were of a particular nature. At the beginning, he did not know if their origin was demonic or divine. His wife convinced him

---

[35] See, *The World's Religions*, edited by Norman Anderson.

[36] Ibid.

[37] See, *The Holy Sword* by Robert Payne.

they were from (Allah) god. Were they audibly heard or were they the product of his own fertile mind? We don't know. The nature of them will forever be a matter of debate. It is said, he may have found them in his heart. He also reports that in his distress and feeling he might be possessed, and while on the way to jump off a cliff, a vision appeared to him in which a voice hailed him as the Apostle of Allah and arrested his suicidal plan. In the same vision, he saw a figure stride the horizon. He stopped, and remained there for some time.[38] At least, we know visions continued over a period of 22 years until his death.[39]

His new faith was not received by all and opposition was encountered, causing him to leave Mecca and flee to Medina. This flight marks in Islamic understanding the beginning of Islam as recorded in Islamic calendars, July 16, 622 (AD). His teachings were, at this stage of his life, rejected by both Jews and Christians. This was the turning point for him to seek Mecca rather than Jerusalem as the center for the new faith.

The Beginnings of Islam in Military Conflict

Soon, he returned to Mecca victorious, having conquered it militarily. This was the beginning of his military career.

Mohammed then systematically quenched all opposition to him and his beliefs, conquering all the surrounding pockets of opposition in Arabia by the sword. His faith then became a political cause as well as a religious cause. Until his death, he extended the boundaries of his religious, and now political,

---

[38] Alfred Guillaume, *Islam*, Penguin Books

[39] See the *Cambridge History of Islam* for further comments.

influence militarily.[40] History reports that as a result, the new faith spread with remarkable speed through the Middle East. All this has set the stage for rightwing Islamist extremists to use military power to also attempt to advance the cause in the name of Allah. The shedding of blood seemed to produce no guilt in his mind.

A marked difference is seen between the life of Jesus and that of Mohammed. Jesus did not take up the sword and urged his disciples to not take the sword. Mohammed took the sword and used it effectively for his cause. The continuing history of Islam is not the purpose of this book.

There are many different sects that have arisen in Islam, with two major divisions: the Sunnis and the Shi'a. Their militant activities have not been limited to unbelievers. They have waged war by shedding blood against each other. Like most faiths, there are extremists; but in this case, Islamic extremists follow the literal words of the Koran when it says to kill unbelievers.[41]

---

[40] See, John B. Noss, *Man's Religions*, MacMillan.

[41] For the words of the Koran on this subject, see the N. J. Dawood's translation of the Koran, London, Penguin Books, 1956, page 333f.

Islam's Beliefs as They Help Us Understand "Who Am I?"

The Five Articles of Faith

These five articles are incumbent on all Muslims to accept and believe.

Allah

The first article of faith is "la, ilaha illa Allah." Translated, it says, "[There is] no god but Allah." Paraphrased, it reads, "There is only one true god and his name is Allah."

From this we conclude that the existence of a divine being for a Muslim is not to be doubted. The same is true of the Judeo-Christian religions.

Next, the distinction between Islam and the Jewish and Christian beliefs about God is made clear by Islam's rejection of the Judeo-Christian God. This is chanted with emphasis in the phrase "la, ilaha illa Allah." It emphatically excludes all understandings of a god that are not Islamic. Therefore, the attributes, nature, and behavior of Allah have been rigidly defined by Islam and no other definitions are true for a Muslim. It also makes clear that who Allah is and who the Judeo-Christian God is are two very different beings.

We also note the use of the word "one" in the Islamic formula. As your understanding of Islamic belief expands, you will be told this means that Jesus cannot be "God the Son" because that, in Islamic thinking, would mean there is more than one god. The Christian doctrine of the Trinity is, as a result, held as untrue. The Islamic understanding of the Triune Christian God, however, is a misunderstanding of Christian belief. For

Islam, no one or thing can be equal to Allah. Allah stands alone! And this last phrase will be significant when it comes to understanding how Islam defines who we are.

Allah is all-powerful, all-seeing, all-hearing, all-willing, transcendent, above everything and everyone else, and the sovereign judge of all mankind. The phrase "all-seeing, all-hearing and all-willing" means his will is final and sovereign. Allah is self-subsistent, meaning he existed before anything else. In other words, he is eternal. He is also the creator. He will also be the final judge of who will be let into paradise (how one enters heaven, for the Christian, bears no resemblance to Islam's teachings about Allah's conditions). This, with the exception of what is in parenthesis, they hold in agreement with the Judeo-Christian beliefs.

Why all this about God? Because what is believed about the divine being will tell us a lot about who we are as understood by these beliefs.

Allah is different from his creatures. Therefore, humans are not made in Allah's image. So great is the transcendence of Allah that it also means the nothingness of everything else in the face of the majesty of Allah[42]. Now we see that the value of a human is greatly reduced in Islam. Destroying a human life is not reprehensible to a Muslim because humans are not made in Allah's image and, therefore, are of a much lesser value. But the taking of a human life is a serious evil to a Christian. This is why Jesus took no life and does not approve of his followers taking up the sword.

In Islamic belief, Allah is so far beyond and removed from humankind in every way that he is *not personally knowable*.

---

[42] Sura 4:171 — Islamic scholar, Seyyed Hossein Nasr

Therefore, the question arises, "In what way is he a person and in what way is our personhood a reflection of his — if he is a person?" Well, he is not a personal god, meaning *not a person*! This and the words in italics (not personally knowable) have the result of lowering the meaning of our personhood and our intrinsic worth. Where did our personhood come from? Islam has no satisfactory answer.

As a result of Allah's transcendence, we have difficulty in finding out much about him at all. From what we see in islamic teachings (and he is not really knowable beyond what Islamic teaching tells us), the probability is that *he is not affected in any way by whatever happens to humankind, yet he is said to be loving* (which is a contradiction of what love is generally thought to be). If he cares, he does not show it. So, what kind of love is that? It is not an overstatement to say that this "loving" aspect of his nature is almost ignored in Islamic teaching. He is supremely a god of justice, and his justice is thought to overrule his love. The dominant theme of Islamic belief is, he is the judge, not the merciful savior; the powerful one, not the God of grace.

Allah stands alone. Therefore, it is difficult to really know him. No-one and no-thing can know him. He is not affected by his creatures — by what they think, feel, or do. There is no intimate relationship with Allah because that, to Islam, would be inconceivable. Allah is, above all else, the judge. So justice is his supreme attribute. Even though Islam admits Allah is love, his love (if it can be known) is lost in the coldness of justice.

Because Allah is alone, unknowable, and unrelated (except as their creator and judge), humans are stripped of what gives them a sense of true value: the value that a god who went to the trouble of creating them shows in his love and his care. If we must think he is our god, he is an aloof, alone, distant, and disinterested one. This should leave his creatures with a sadness in the pit of their stomach and with no sense of self-worth beyond their achievements — even beyond the sense of worth their obedience to all the ritualistic and moral requirements laid on them by Islamic practices brings them. Muslims are in the same boat as all the philosophies and religions that exclude a God who is a person. They are living a life without value beyond what they create for themselves.

All humans are left, in Islamic belief, to find significance in their actions and attitudes. And if they fail, their failed actions rob then of all the value they have. Simply put, Islam attributes no real intrinsic value to a human apart from their obedience to what Allah demands of them. The idea that the god of Islam is also a god of love means extremely little. Man, in his grasping for a better foundation on which to feel worthy and valuable, is left very disappointed. So, in a different way to the other faiths we have surveyed, Islam also ends up reducing our intrinsic value to nothing. Allah is by no means the God of the Judeo-Christian religions, of course.

The god of Islam, if loving, makes us ask, "How? Why?" Islam wants us to fear Allah, the great judge, and when fear is the sum of a relationship, there is no sense of love in the relationship. Respect, maybe. There is no reason to love Allah if he does not demonstrate his love to us in return. Love is only complete if it is given both ways — a mutual experience. We never continue to love someone who does not return our love if we want to feel loved. Allah is like the remote god of Hinduism and acts like the "no god" of Buddhism. He may as well not be called loving.

Here is a killer. Allah is also the source of both good and evil[43] and whatever he decides is right. It is therefore impossible to form an ethical statement of what is right and wrong for humans, because whatever Allah chooses is right — meaning there is no standard for right and wrong beyond what he wills. That is meaningless if he is both good and evil. The difference between good and evil is obliterated. It leaves the possibility that he can be a very capricious god and, given the fact that he is the source of both evil and good, we are left to wonder what he might decide next. His will is supreme, remember — no self-accountability for him. And none that he may impose on himself can be regarded as consistent in his nature.[44]

So how is he reliably a just judge? How do we know that anything he has promised will come true? Evil is not known for keeping its promises. Who would want a relationship with a god like that?

Islam has many similarities to Christianity, sharing some of the Jewish and Christian Scriptures, for example. But what it accepts and rejects of the Jewish and Christian Scriptures creates great differences. It edits them severely. These differences produce very opposite results for humans from what Christianity practices, as is easily seen in Islam's treatment of women. Although Shari'a is the practical law for

---

[43] This belief has been central to Islam's teaching and is called Kismet, the decrees of Allah, which are one's fate. It is fatalistic and has been said to be the reason behind the lack of drive to better oneself and make something of oneself among some Muslims. Who am I? is a matter for Allah's will, our fate.

[44] There is a complete accountability in the Judeo-Christian God because he has bound himself by his promises, by his word and his faithfulness.

daily living and is undergoing some modification to make it more acceptable to the modern world, it is still in deep conflict with the Christian Scriptures, and its basic doctrines diverge to create a religion that in no way could be confused with Christianity. Women are not honored as equal to men.

Even though they claim to have four sacred writings (the Torah, Psalms, Gospel of Christ, and the Koran), they maintain that all but the Koran have been corrupted, leaving the Koran as the only errorless sacred book. That neatly does away with anything in their other sacred scriptures that they don't like.

In Islam, the question "Who am I" is answered a little differently from the other Eastern religions — in fact, all religions. It gives us no value; we have to create our own. And it equates our value with our obedience to Allah, who is both good and evil. The evil is seen in the way it dispatches with unbelievers when it chooses to do so.

It is even blasphemous to call Allah "Father," for example. We are intrinsically part of the worthlessness and nothingness when we stand before Allah. Everything apart from Allah is valued as nothingness. We are included in that statement. Islam is closer to Hinduism than Christianity. To be a person is to have the qualities of personhood[45] that create the need

---

[45] The qualities of personhood require the ability to love. If god is one (a singularity of person), as Islam maintains (Islam denies the Christian concept of the Trinity — one being, God in three persons), then before the creation of the world, God would have had no opportunity to express his love. Love is real only in its expression. This is not the discussion here, but a God that is one God in three persons (which seems so hard to understand) is the only way God could have been existent as the God of love before the creation of the world. This is the God of Christianity that is taught in the Bible and not the god of any other religion.

for and the beauty of relationships. Relationships interact, give of themselves, bask in each other's attention, and reward each other. All of this is lacking in Islam without Allah being a person.

Angels

A further cause for concern about who we are is in the actions of angels. Islam believes in angels — both good and evil ones. Everyone is assigned two recording angels: one to record our good deeds and the other, our bad deeds. Just imagine this: one angel on each shoulder and never absent. What is concerning is, there is never a chance for us to expect any change in the record. A bad deed cannot be redacted. The unstated purpose of this assignment of angels seems to be to assure good behavior. Its effect could also be quite demotivating for imperfect human beings who struggle with controlling bad habits.

Where are grace and forgiveness, and a God "remembering our sins no more"? In Islam, I am set up for an infallible recording of my failures. In the Christian understanding of God, I can find forgiveness and have the record declare "your sins are remembered no more." In Islam, there is no second chance to show my obedience. Because we are imperfect beings, we are in need of a way of salvation from our errors and sins.

Scriptures

We have covered the Islamic beliefs about the supremacy of the Koran. I have issues with the Koran. Not least is the approval of killing unbelievers.[46] If this is encouraged (and it is), "What is a human's worth as a human?" we must ask again. In Islam, humans are creatures whose value is non existent if they don't agree to believe and follow the Islamic articles of faith. And if they do believe and follow, in the end they are a part of the nothingness that exists outside of Allah. That doubles down on humans having no intrinsic value.

Prophets

This Articles of Faith say nothing directly about our worth as humans.

The Last Days

Its timing is a secret, but there are 25 signs that will precede the approach of the last days. At the end, everyone will be raised from the dead and the angels' books will be opened. Allah will weigh the deeds of each person, and those allowed into Paradise will recline on soft couches, drinking wine that is handed to them by the Maidens of Paradise, who they can marry — as many of these maidens as they please. Those whose bad deeds outweighed the good deeds will be sent to Hell.

---

[46] Islamic teachers have tried to handle the task of explaining away these statements found in the Koran. They give them an interpretive twist. But how can that be done in the face of Mohammed signing off on an assassination and having the blood of many on his own hands (from his conquests of other tribes who resisted his teachings and his authority because of their disbelief in them)? It is a literal reading of his own writings in the Koran that authorizes his followers to amputate and burn nonbelievers at the stake. Are the Isis murderers, who killed so many in the name of Allah, not also doing what their infallible prophet taught and did himself?

Again, value is declared by our deeds alone, and the story of no intrinsic value, no love, no forgiveness, no grace, no mercy in life is sealed.

According to Islam, Who Am I?

So, who am I? Even though I have a creator, he is divorced from his creation and I am left as though I don't matter and to find my worth only in my deeds, which are never perfect. I am left with a failed search for a self-respect that lifts me above the dismal realization of my failures. We long to feel important and unique, to be loved for the person of value that we are by the one we worship. Sorry, no hope here.

✶ ✶ ✶ ✶ ✶

All these faiths, including Islam, fall short of giving us a solid foundation for intrinsic self-worth. Don't forget, all people believe something. So the real question is "What does your belief do to your self-worth?" Our deeds are imperfect and change, so if we have lasting value it must come from elsewhere. Where? The source of our being must be a person who thinks, loves, and is our infallible guide through life, or we have no intrinsic value. And if we are distinct from all the animals and are made in the image of our creator-source (who is a person — only Christianity fulfills all we crave to feel worthy, important, and valuable[47]), we have intrinsic value and can love ourselves despite our imperfections and failures. If the Creator God gives us this intrinsic value and also loves us for the unique individual that we are, we live with the feeling of worth we long for: to be loved . We also can love and be loved by that creator-person, God.

---

[47] So far, I have bracketed Judaism and Christianity together under the title, Judeo-Christian religions. The one is under the first covenant between God and man and the second covenant refers to what is commonly called the New Testament. A testament is a covenant, and the Christian Bible contains both the Old Testament and the New Testament. The covenants are not contradictory, but the second is the fulfillment of the first and contains the greatest display of God's love for us in the sacrifice of Christ on the cross and his resurrection. The death of Christ alone, without the resurrection, would convey a false message of God's love. Ending in death, God's love would have failed. Instead, God's love is victorious over all evil and death. There is no end point to his love. Reflecting on this, Paul says (speaking of divine love which we are to seek to imitate), "…Love [as seen in God] never fails!" (1Corinthians 13:8).

Conclusion

You have begun the first and most important task in your mission to be straight thinkers: namely, to learn how to think straight and combat the insurgence of crooked thinking in our culture and in our world. If we become passive victims of this crooked way of thinking, we promote it. If we remain silent, we also give it credence.

Our thinking is the inner castle of our minds. We build that castle with thoughts that are either governed by the practice of correct and rational thinking or with crooked and deceitful arguments. What we think is who we are. When our thinking has no true north and no guidelines or even desire for truth, we cause ourselves grief and guilt. Happiness is never found in the dishonesty of crooked, deceit ridden thinking. If you have a desire to be a straight thinker and reject all temptations to fall in line with the half-truths that entice the unthinking, then accept the challenge to build a mind that you are proud of. Those who fall for the enticing appeal of a life that is free to do what they please will play fast and loose with the facts, treasure lies, and die to goodness. This cancer of the mind grows fast, so become discerning thinkers and lovers of all that is true and good.

We always start by becoming aware of what is dishonest and deceptive. Then, we apply the rules of straight thinking. We do not live to ourselves and, therefore, we exert an influence in our world for truth or dishonesty by how we think. Those of us who attempt to live and think with integrity will leave a lasting legacy for those who follow us. It is a humbling thought, but we have only one life to live and although we can't undo our mistakes, we can be forgiven and redirect our course. So accept God's forgiveness and finish the race with confidence and integrity — both a head and heart faith.

So much of what this book has attempted to expose is nothing more than apocryphal, deliberate duplicity. You have in this book a template to set out confidently on the road to right and truth. All things start in the mind and we can only become transformed by the renewing of our minds.

✻ ✻ ✻ ✻ ✻

No doubt, if you are a parent, you have already started the task of helping your child think straight. Just as important is teaching them to detect the crooked thinking all around them. It can be fun guiding the development of their virile minds. If *you* don't, *others* will.

A mind is the most precious thing your child has. A mind doesn't naturally understand what is best for it, nor how it must function to excel. It depends on gaining the right knowledge and learning how to think straight, which is where the parent comes in. The mind of a child absorbs everything it sees, hears, and experiences. Dropping what will not be of use or will actually limit their mind's effectiveness (like crooked thinking) is the task of the child, together with the aid of those they believe and respect. They need to learn straight thinking from someone. Best they learn it from you. A parent's lack of guidance tells them that what is overlooked is of no or little importance. The educational system, or their peers, even their peer's parents can turn them into crooked thinkers.

Parenting is not just teaching them how to brush their teeth and bathe, but how to use their minds effectively. Teach them the difference between straight and crooked thinking and their minds will eclipse those of their peers. So start using the tools I have given you to make lasting impressions and shape in their minds the only honest ways to think.

There is a lot to absorb and lock into your thinking, as well. So read again the sections you feel are most helpful. Train your own mind so that you can combat all the crooked thinking and deliberate deceptions blatantly flaunted in today's world. Give your children beliefs their heads can defend, the ones they need to be able to live with conviction. Christians know where to find those proven beliefs. What is needed is the knowledge of how to defend them and show their superiority.

Enter into the thoughts of their minds so that you know them better and understand the young person God has given you. Most of the struggles a parent has with their child is because they do not understand how the child is wired and the needs of their temperament that will shape their lives.

Their temperament is most likely not the same as yours. Therefore, I strongly suggest parents complete the Adult Temperament Key to understand the urges and drives that are shaping their own lives and to realize how this is affecting their parenting of their child. All the strengths of each temperament are good but, at times, different from what drives another temperament. Next, complete the Child Temperament Key (for ages 2-12) to better understand your child from the very beginning. For teenagers, begin using the Adult Temperament Key annually, offering your explanation where needed to augment their lack of life experience. Make sure to let them answer according to how *they* feel about themselves. There are no wrong answers. You will see the changes in their self-understanding as the teenage years unfold, which will increase your knowledge of how they are progressively understanding themselves.

*[You will find both the Adult Temperament Key and the Child Temperament Key reprinted for you in Appendix I and Appendix II, respectively. Or you can complete the Adult Temperament Key online, where it is scored for you at **https://raywlincoln.com/temperament-key** Just be sure to take a screenshot of the results it provides at the end, or write down your results, and save the information for future reference. A copy of the Child Temperament Key can be downloaded for your convenience as well at **https://raywlincoln.lpages.co/oi-childkey**.]*

Once the temperament keys are completed, review the descriptions of the four temperaments in Appendix III to verify your results.

When these steps have been completed, I suggest you purchase and read either *I'm a Keeper* (for parenting through ages 10 or 12) or *INNERKINETICS* (for parenting teens, and it's also for all adults) and continue your understanding of your child at a deeper level. You will be thankful for the knowledge their temperament gives that can translate into very significant and practical help for your parenting.

If you start training their minds to think straight from the beginning, you will be way ahead of the game. From birth to six or thereabouts, the child's mind is very malleable. These are the formative years. Use the simplest applications of the tools and they will not forget them easily. Then parent them according to how they have been designed. "I don't know what to do," is the cry of most parents, and only because they have not yet understood how their child has been uniquely made. Understanding their temperament will be your guide to what to do.

Make all your training fun for yourself and your child. Treat your children's minds with even greater importance than their bodies. The mind controls the body!

Sincerely
Ray W. Lincoln

Appendices

Appendix I — The InnerKinetics Temperament Key for Adults

(Reprinted from INNERKINETICS — Your Blueprint to Excellence and Happiness)

Instructions:
Both the Adult Temperament Key and Child Temperament Key used here have been developed using the principles of research into temperament that Myers/Briggs, Keirsey and Harkey/Jourgensen have used for the development of their assessments. These principles, when used in assessments, have proved very reliable and can be depended upon. Any of the above named assessments of temperament are excellent guides to the discovery of how you are made on the inside.

As long as you carefully follow the instructions for each of the Temperament Keys, you should get excellent results.

This is a very positive assessment. We are looking for your strengths, not your weaknesses. There are no wrong answers since it is a self-assessment. However, be as accurate as possible. Read these instructions carefully since a knowledgeable guide is not looking over your shoulder and you can't ask for help. <u>It is imperative that you answer according to these instructions.</u>

- Answer these questions according to your preferences (what you prefer), not according to how you think others would have you answer.
- Answer each question individually. Don't try to be consistent.
- Aim to get through the key in about 20 minutes or less.
- Think carefully about each answer, but avoid over-thinking, which can lead to confusion. If you are over-thinking, ask yourself, "What am I the most?"
- Again, let me put it this way: You will see yourself as both (a) and (b) in some of the questions. Your answer should be what you see yourself to <u>be</u> the <u>most</u>, or what you <u>prefer</u> the <u>most.</u>

- Your preferences are often different at home than at work. This can be due to the fact that, at work, certain things are required of you. Therefore, they have become your work preferences. You prefer to do it that way at work since that's what is good for you. If your work preferences differ from your home preferences, answer according to your home preferences.
- We want to know what really beats in your breast, what really satisfies, fulfills, or pleases you the most.

The results should be accurate. But if you attend one of my seminars, ask to be checked again. It's a service we provide. When you read the descriptions of the temperaments that are provided at the end (also in *I'm a Keeper* or *INNERKINETICS),* you will determine whether they match your resulting letters from the temperament key. If they do not match the descriptions, then you answered with something else in mind, and you will need to switch to the temperament that describes what is most like you.

This check on your answers is very helpful. The ones who are most likely to be confused about themselves are the NFs. They are the complicated temperament and have the greatest difficulties in understanding themselves for that understandable reason. Now, proceed with careful thought.

Check "A" or "B" for each question. Please answer ALL questions.

1. At social gatherings, do you prefer to

_____ A. Socialize with everyone
_____ B. Stick to your friends

2. Are you more in touch with

_____ A. The real world
_____ B. The world inside your mind; the world of possibilities

3. Do you rely more on, or take more notice of

_____ A. Your experiences
_____ B. Your hunches/gut feelings

4. Are you (most of the time)

_____ A. Cool, calm and collected
_____ B. Friendly and warm

5. When evaluating people do you tend to be

_____ A. Impersonal and frank
_____ B. Personal and considerate

6. Do you mostly feel a sense of

_____ A. Urgency/upset if you are not on time
_____ B. Relaxed about time

7. When you see a mess, do you

_____ A. Have an urge to tidy it up
_____ B. Feel reasonably comfortable living with it

8. Would you describe yourself as

_____ A. Outgoing/ demonstrative/easy to approach
_____ B. Somewhat reserved/private

9. Which are you best at

_____ A. Focusing on details
_____ B.Catching the big picture, the connections, the patterns

10. Children should be

_____ A. Made to be more responsible
_____ B. Encouraged to exercise their imagination and make-believe more

11. When making decisions, are you more influenced by

_____ A. The facts. impersonal data
_____ B. Personal feelings

12. Do you feel more yourself when giving

_____ A. Honest criticism
_____ B. Support, approval, and encouragement

13. Do you work best

_____ A. Scheduled; to deadlines
_____ B. Unscheduled; no deadline

14. For a vacation, do you prefer to

_____ A. Plan ahead of time
_____ B. Choose as you go

15. When you are with others do you usually

_____ A. Initiate the conversation
_____ B. Listen and tend to be slow to speak

16. Most of the time, facts

_____ A. Should be taken at face value
_____ B. Suggest ideas, possibilities, or principles

17. Do you mostly feel

_____ A. In touch with the real world
_____ B. Somewhat removed

18. When in an argument/ discussion, do you care more about

_____ A. Defending your position and being right
_____ B. Finding harmony and agreement

19. With others, do you tend to be

_____ A. Firm
_____ B. Gentle

20. Do you see yourself as

_____ A. Predictable
_____ B. Unpredictable

21. Do you mostly prefer to

_____ A. Get things done; come to closure
_____ B. Explore alternatives; keep options open

22. After two hours at a party, are you

_____ A. More energized than when you arrived
_____ B. Losing your energy

250

23. Which best describes you

_____ A. Down to earth, practical
_____ B. Imaginative, an idea person

24. Which do you finally rely on more

_____ A. Common sense
_____ B. Your intuition/insights or your own analysis

25. In other people, which appeals to you most

_____ A. A strong will
_____ B. Warm emotions

26. Are you more controlled by

_____ A. Your head/thought
_____ B. Your heart/emotions

27. Are you typically

_____ A. Eager to get decisions made
_____ B. Not keen on making decisions

28. On the whole, do you spend your money

_____ A. Cautiously
_____ B. Impulsively

29. When you have lost energy, do you find yourself mostly

_____ A. Seeking out people
_____ B. Seeking out solitude/ a quiet corner

30. Do dreamers

_____ A. Annoy you somewhat
_____ B. Fascinate and interest you

31. Do you rely more

_____ A. On your five senses
_____ B. On your sixth sense/ intuition

32. Are you more

_____ A. Tough-minded
_____ B. Tender-hearted

33. Would you more likely choose to be

_____ A. Truthful
_____ B. Tactful

34. Do you see yourself as more

_____ A. Serious and determined
_____ B. Relaxed and easygoing

35. Do you feel more comfortable when

_____ A. Things are decided
_____ B. Your options are still open

251

36. Would you say you mostly

_____ A. Show your feelings readily

_____ B. Are private about your feelings and keep them inside

37. Would you prefer

_____ A. To be in touch with reality

_____ B. To exercise a creative imagination

38. Is your way of thinking more

_____ A. Conventional
_____ B. Original and creative

39. What motivates you more

_____ A. Solid evidence
_____ B. An emotional appeal

40. Would you rather be known for

_____ A. Being a consistent thinker

_____ B. Having harmonious relationships

41. Do you tend to

_____ A. Value routines
_____ B. Dislike routines

42. Do you live more with

_____ A. A little sense of urgency
_____ B. A leisurely pace

43. Do you have

_____ A. Many friends and count them all your close friends

_____ B. Few friends, and only one or two that are deep friends

44. Do you place more emphasis on what you see

_____ A. With your physical eyes

_____ B. With your mind's eye

45. Are you

_____ A Thick skinned; not hurt easily

_____ B. Thin skinned; hurt easily

46. When you are asked to create a "To Do" list, does it

_____ A. Seem like the right thing to do and feel it will be helpful

_____ B. Bug you and seem more like an unnecessary chore

47. Which word attracts you most or describes you best?

_____ A. Talkative
_____ B. Quiet

48. Which words attract you most or describe you best?

_____ A. Present realities
_____ B. Future hopes

49. Which word(s) attracts you most or describe(s) you best?

_____ A. Logic
_____ B. Loving heart

50. Which word attracts you most or describes you best?

_____ A. Plan
_____ B. Impulse

51. Which word attracts you most or describes you best?

_____ A. Party
_____ B. Home

52. Which word(s) attracts you most or describe(s) you best?

_____ A. Common sense
_____ B. Vision

53. Which word attracts you most or describes you best?
_____ A. Justice
_____ B. Mercy

54. Which word attracts you most or describes you best?

_____ A. Concerned
_____ B. Carefree

SCORE SHEET INSTRUCTIONS

1. Place a X in the appropriate column (A or B) to indicate the answer you chose for each numbered question. **[Please note that the numbers run from left to right across the chart.]**

2. Count the number of "As" in column #1 and write that number in box "c," above the "E."   Count the number of "Bs" in column #1 and write that number in box "d," above the "I."

3. Count the number of "As" in column #2 and write that number in box "e." Count the number of "Bs" in column #2 and write that number in box "f."

4. Count the number of "As" in column #3 and write that number in box "g." Count the number of "Bs" in column #3 and write that number in box "h."

5. Add the number of "As" for columns 2 and 3 together and write the total in box "i."   Add the number of "Bs" for columns 2 and 3 and write that number in box "j."

6. Repeat the steps in instructions 3-5 above for columns 4/5 and 6/7.

7. Which did you have more of, "Es" or "Is"? _____
    Which did you have more of, "Ss" or "Ns"? _____
    Which did you have more of, "Ts" or "Fs"? _____
    Which did you have more of, "Js" or "Ps"? _____

8. In the four letters you listed in Instruction #7 (the ones you got the most of), which two-letter combination below is present? Circle it!

    S and P   S and J   N and T   N and F

	1		2		3		4		5		6		7	
	A	B	A	B	A	B	A	B	A	B	A	B	A	B
1			2		3		4		5		6		7		
8			9		10		11		12		13		14		
15			16		17		18		19		20		21		
22			23		24		25		26		27		28		
29			30		31		32		33		34		35		
36			37		38		39		40		41		42		
43			44				45				46				
47			48				49				50				
51			52				53				54				

					g	h			m	n			s	t
					e	f			k	l			q	r
	c	d			l	j			o	p			u	v
	E	**I**			**S**	**N**			**T**	**F**			**J**	**P**

255

Follow These Steps to Finalize Your Temperament Identification

1. Read the descriptions of the temperaments that follow and select the temperament that is most like you. You may find that not all the aspects of a temperament truly reflect who you are. That's not uncommon. We are individuals and all are a little different, so what you are looking for is which of the four descriptions fits you best. Which is most like you?

2. You may find that you see a little of yourself in several or all of the temperaments. Don't worry. We all imitate others and therefore "borrow" strengths and characteristics from other temperaments for many reasons, not least to meet what others demand of us. What we need to know is which temperament we really are? As the research indicates we are one temperament, not a mixture of temperaments, and those glimpses of ourselves in other temperaments are simply our adopted strengths. Borrowed strengths or characteristics are just that, borrowed. Our own strengths are the ones that satisfy and fulfill us when we use them. We must know them.

3. Does the one that fits you best agree with your temperament key results? The two letters of the temperament you have chosen must occur in the four letters that your temperament key gave you. If they do, no further decision is needed.

4. If they don't, then you can go back and check your answers to the temperament key. Are they really what your preferences are and not what others have led you to believe you are or what you would like to be based on expectations others have given you? Make sure you answered the questions as instructed. A small number of people who take the temperament key may find it doesn't seem to ring true

with who they perceive they are from reading the descriptions. If so, go with what you perceive is the temperament that fits you best.

Appendix II — The InnerKinetics Child Temperament Key

PLEASE PRINT OUT A COPY OF THIS DOCUMENT FOR EACH CHILD.

PART A: Is Your Child an "E" or an "I"? (Extroversion versus Introversion). Please circle the letter of the appropriate choice, "A" or "B," for your child. **Once you have completed these 17 questions, please transfer your "A" or "B" answers to "Score Sheet A" below.**

1. Is your child normally
   A. Outgoing and engaging
   B. Reserved and quiet

2. Does your child
   A. Approach people and things seemingly without hesitation, head erect
   B. Hesitate and hold back when faced with unfamiliar people and things, dropping their head and acting a little shy

3. Does your child
   A. Tend to gain energy in the company of other children
   B. Tend to become drained after a period and lose energy, stand on the side and take breaks from the energy center, or seek adult company

4. Did your child
   A. Develop good social skills quickly
   B. Develop good social skills slowly or not yet

5. Does your child
   A. Love to be on the phone with strangers and seem animated when on the phone
   B. Show shyness and reserve when on the phone to a stranger

259

6. Does your child
    A. Chat naturally with other people, particularly other children, when in line at a grocery store
    B. Keep close to you and try not to be seen or spoken to

7. Is your child
    A. Rather talkative in the company of others
    B. One who tends to listen and talk only after gathering confidence

8. Is your child
    A. Easy to approach
    B. Difficult to draw out

9. Does your child
    A. Respond quickly when asked to do something or when asked a question
    B. Respond slowly, as though he or she is musing over the request and as though he or she is trying to figure it out; or as though he or she is stubborn and doesn't want to respond

10. Does your child seem to
    A. Have no secrets
    B. Hold part of themselves in reserve, hidden from public view

11. Does your child tend to
    A. Seek and need the company of others
    B. Enjoy solitude and play alone happily

12. Does your child attempt making friends
    A. Easily and openly
    B. Cautiously and selectively

13. Would your child prefer
    A. A noisy environment
    B. A quiet, more subdued environment

14. Does a new environment with new people
    A. Seem to excite your child
    B. Seem to stress your child

15. Does a house full of people
    A. Bring your child out of hiding
    B. Cause your child to retreat to his or her room

16. For your child, is becoming the focus of attention
    A. Exciting
    B. Embarrassing

17. Which pair of words describes your child best?
    A. Outgoing, approachable
    B. Reserved, shy

Score Sheet A

Q#	Name	
	A	B
1		
2		
3		
4		
5		
6		
7		
8		
9		
10		
11		
12		
13		
14		
15		
16		
17		
Total		

Count the A's and B's. The higher score indicates part of your child's type. More "As" indicates that your child is an "E" (extrovert); more "Bs" indicates an "I" (introvert).

PART B: IS YOUR CHILD AN "S" OR AN "N"? (Sensing versus Intuitive)

This is the hardest of the four categories to determine due to the difficulty of relying on observation alone when we are determining the child's internal perception. At an early age, only the extreme N's can be spotted. If you are doubtful in your responses to the following questions, you may have to wait until age three or four before you can identify with accuracy.

Please circle the letter of the appropriate choice, "A" or "B," for your child. **Once you have completed these 17 questions, please transfer your "A" or "B" answers to "Score Sheet B" below.**

1. Does your child prefer
   A. Action to stories
   B. Stories to action

2. Does your child prefer
   A. Down-to-earth, real life stories about things that are familiar
   B. Imaginative tales full of fanciful characters and larger than life heroes (Fairy tales like: *Jack in the Beanstalk, Cinderella, Star Wars,* and songs like *Puff the Magic Dragon*)

3. Does your child
   A. Bounce up ready to go to play when the story is over, or even before
   B. Plead for you to read more or to read it again

4. In picture books, does your child
   A. Prefer the simple, bold, graphic illustration
   B. Prefer the detailed, rich and colorful pictures

5. Does your child
   A. Seem always to be focused on the real world in their play (their toys, things and people around them)
   B. Daydream often, make up imaginative characters, or weave fanciful stories into their play (making their toys whatever the story wants them to be, and seem hungry for fantasy)

6. Does your child
   A. Seem to be an average child, getting upset and then getting over their upset like you would expect
   B. Remain hurt for long periods and/or hate passionately and seem to be able to hurt skillfully and put his finger on your vulnerable spot (push your buttons)

7. If the toy he is playing with is a truck
   A. Is it always a truck?
   B. Is it sometimes a submarine, an airplane, or a monster (but seldom a truck?)

8. When you break a promise to your child (i.e. "Sorry, we can't go to the zoo as promised"), does he (or she)
   A. Get upset and get over it reasonably quickly
   B. Get deeply hurt and take a long time to get over it

9. Would you say that your child is
   A. Comparatively easy to handle
   B. Difficult to handle

10. Does your child seem
    A. Normal
    B. Strangely different from other children

11. There are two ways to answer this question. Answer the question that is based on **YOUR** temperament.

If YOU (the parent) are a very practical, down to earth person **(SP or SJ)** answer this: Does your child
    A. Seem like you
    B. Bewilder you; and do you find yourself often getting angry with your child out of frustration

If YOU (the parent) are an **NT or an NF**, answer this: Does your child
    A. Seem NOT to be like you
    B. Seem like you

12. Has your child had any strange premonitions or the like?
    A. No
    B. Yes

13. Would your child be likely to have an imaginary friend?
    A. No
    B. Yes

14. What does your child focus on most?
    A. Today and its excitements
    B. Tomorrow and its possibilities

15. Does your child's mind
    A. Function as a database
    B. Bubble with ideas

16. Do you see your child growing up to be comfortable in
    A. The world of facts and figures, the real world
    B. The world of imagination, ideas and books

17. Which pair of words describes your child best?
    A. Organized, realistic
    B. Insightful, imaginative

Score Sheet B

Q#	Name	
	A	B
1		
2		
3		
4		
5		
6		
7		
8		
9		
10		
11		
12		
13		
14		
15		
16		
17		
Total		

Count the A's and B's. The higher score indicates part of your child's type. More "As" indicates that your child is an "S" (sensor); more "Bs" indicates an "N" (intuitive).

PART C: IS YOUR CHILD A "T" OR AN "F"? (Thinking versus Feeling)

This one should not be too hard now that you have the routine down.

Please circle the letter of the appropriate choice, "A" or "B," for your child. **Once you have completed these 17 questions, please transfer your "A" or "B" answers to "Score Sheet C" below.**

1. Does your child
    A. Always want a reason, always ask "why," and never seem happy with "because I said so" (obviously an extra curious type)
    B. Express normal curiosity, not ask why continuously, accept most things at face value

2. Does your child seem
    A. Impervious to getting his feelings hurt
    B. To get his feelings hurt very easily

3. Does your child
    A. Give the impression that he or she doesn't favor being touched and appreciates it less than you expect
    B. Loves being touched

4. Is your child
    A. Reserved about sitting close to you and touching you, does your child seem as though he or she doesn't need closeness and touching?
    B. One who cuddles easily and always wants to touch you?

5. Would you say your child
    A. Has difficulty with showing affection to others
    B. Is the real affectionate type

6. Does your child normally
    A. Show little expressiveness and feeling
    B. Show frequent expressiveness with his emotions.

7. Would you say your child
    A. Seems to live just for himself
    B. Wants to please adults and shows a strong concern to please them

8. Has it been
    A.   A long time since your child performed a little service for you and showed that he was looking for your approval and appreciation
    B. Only a short while since your child performed one of these little services, frequently touching your heart

9. Is your child
    A. A cool and even-tempered child (more of a cerebral child)
    B. An emotionally warm-hearted, friendly child (more about the heart than the head)

10. Is your child
    A. More firm than gentle
    B. More gentle than firm

11. Does your child seem
    A. Unaffected by sad endings to stories
    B. To obviously prefer happy endings

12. Unless angered, is your child
    A. Straight forward, even blunt, in representing the truth
    B. Careful not to hurt the feelings of others

13. Do you think your child would
    A. Enjoy debate and argument
    B. Prefer to be a peacemaker

14. Which pair of words best describes your child
    A. Strong-minded, winning
    B. Kind, forgiving

15. Which would please your child most
    A. Being praised for excelling over others
    B. Being praised for being kind

16. Which might touch your child most
    A. Reason
    B. Emotion

17. Would your child be more likely to
    A. Praise the winner
    B. Comfort the loser

Score Sheet C

Q#	Name	
	A	B
1		
2		
3		
4		
5		
6		
7		
8		
9		
10		
11		
12		
13		
14		
15		
16		
17		
Total		

Count the A's and B's. The higher score indicates part of your child's type. More "As" indicates that your child is an "T" (thinker); more "Bs" indicates an "F" (feeler).

PART D: IS YOUR CHILD a "J" or a "P"? (Likes things decided or likes to keep things open).

This is the last set of questions to round out your child's personality profile.

Please circle the letter of the appropriate choice, "A" or "B," for your child. **Once you have completed these 17 questions, please transfer your "A" or "B" answers to "Score Sheet D" below.**

1. Does your child
    - A. Tend to be ready for school on time and get worried about being late
    - B. Appear indifferent about being late and mostly shows little concern

2. Are your child's closets and drawers
    - A. Comparatively neat and orderly (for a child)
    - B. Better described as a "rat's nest" (Does he show signs of not understanding why mother is upset about it?)

3. Does your child
    - A. Show signs of wanting his life settled and in order, preferring routines; in fact gets disturbed when routines are changed
    - B. Show little concern about changes to routines and seems to let things just happen in any way; chafes at routines, and is rather happy-go-lucky

4. Does your child
    - A. Like decisions made quickly, can't stand to be in limbo
    - B. Prefer to procrastinate and keep all options open, putting decisions off

5. Does your child tend to
    - A. Run the activities of other children
    - B. Accept what everyone is doing, or plays as he or she pleases in a group of children

6. Is your child
    A. Always making "for sure" statements as though he or she knows everything for sure (exaggerates)
    B. Seldom a user of an exaggerated degree of certainty in their speech

7. Does your child show
    A. Respect for rules and regulations
    B. An indifference to the established rules unless he made them himself

8. Does your child show
    A. A contentedness to be like other children
    B. That he wants to be different in some unusual way

9. Does your child
    A. Wake up, get dressed, usually without being reminded to dress
    B. Need to be reminded constantly to get up and get dressed

10. Does your child wake up and
    A. Want to know what is happening that day
    B. Show little concern and is happy to let things happen as they unfold

11. Would you describe your child's style of living as
    A. More hurried
    B. More leisurely

12. Would you describe your child's style of living as
    A. More deliberate
    B. More spontaneous

13. Would you say your child is more
    A. Meticulous and particular about things
    B. Free-wheeling and casual about things

14. Is your child more
    A. Directed
    B. Changeable

15. Does your child
   A. Want to get things done, want to come to closure
   B. Want to keep things open-ended; seem not to be in a hurry

16. When your child cleans up his or her own room
   A. Is your child neat about it
   B. Does he or she show little care for organization

17. Does your child tend to
   A. Safely store all treasured items
   B. Get distracted easily and not complete the task

Score Sheet D

Q#	Name	
	A	B
1		
2		
3		
4		
5		
6		
7		
8		
9		
10		
11		
12		
13		
14		
15		
16		
17		
Total		

Count the A's and B's. The higher score indicates part of your child's type. More "As" indicates that your child is a "J"; more "Bs" indicates a "P".

Now write the four letters that received the highest scores on the four blanks below:

(Example: Lynda — ESTP). This is your child's personality **type** (one type of a possible 16).

_____ _____ _____ _____

NEXT, do you have in the four letters your Child's results an S and a P **OR** an S and a J **OR** an N and a T, **OR** an N and an F? Write the two-letter combination below that occurs in the four-letter combinations for your child. This is the child's **temperament**. Your child will be one of four temperaments: SP, SJ, NT, or NF.

_____ _____

Remember: When assessing a child's type or temperament, we must remain somewhat tentative — not that the child's temperament will change — but because the child can't provide us with feedback to our questions about the internalization of his or her thoughts and feelings. However, you can proceed with confidence since inaccurate assessments are rather rare.

Appendix III — The Four Temperaments Briefly Described

SP

They crave action, excitement, and stimulation, be it in sport, physical skills with the use of tools of all kinds, the performing arts, or even fine art. They are after a "good time" and only the introverted ones can happily sit still. SPs love freedom and act spontaneously. Therefore, they do not take to authority with relish. Possessing a natural talent for all things physical, they can be the world's playmates. They are lovable, exciting, adventuresome, and brave risk-takers. SPs are pleasant, tactical, and squeeze the last drop of excitement out of each moment. Adaptable, carefree, optimistic, individualistic, they crave self expression. Tolerance accompanies competitiveness and a generous spirit is usually seen in them.

Does this describe you best?

SJ

They are hard-working (many are workaholics) with a responsible work ethic and they crave a feeling of security, which makes them somewhat cautious in their adventures. They coined the motto "Be prepared," and they like everything in order. Home, family, and responsibilities, all cast around rules and regulations. This makes them feel comfortable. They are the solid citizens and the backbone of society. They feel a sense of duty and feel drawn to be useful (helpmates). If someone does not do their duty it irks them.

Change can be unnerving and security is paramount if they are to be happy. They are more conservative than the SP and they like to feel in control of their world. They tend more to worry and pessimism rather than an optimistic attitude that all will be well. They must struggle to ensure all is well. Their nature is more serious and they are the guardians of society.

Does this describe you best?

NT

We could call this one the ingenious/technology temperament, although everyone craves the benefits of technology these days. They are curious and inventive, often finding their way into science and engineering occupations. NTs want to understand everything and build things. Often they are driven and compulsive, but display few people skills naturally. They are hardworking if what they are doing interests them. Feelings are not worn on the surface. NTs want to find new ways of doing things.

Facts, theories, strategies fill their minds and fuel their determination and focus. All things logical and only what makes sense guides them. They must feel independent, calm, cool, and intelligent. Scientific inquiry, mathematical, precision, and logical consistency in a skeptical mind describes them well. NTs are mindmates.

Does this describe you best?

NF

They care very deeply about people and their world and want to lead people to their potential and to feelings of wholeness. NFs are very passionate, tender, loving, soulmates who want to please. Their inner world is frustrated with struggles, and they are the influencers of society, often finding their way into higher education (as do the NTs) and into teaching, counseling, and personal growth. They champion causes that benefit society and provide for the betterment of humankind. They long to better themselves together with the aforementioned urge to help others be all that they can be. They are emotionally rich and complicated and are easily hurt, with their emotions very near the surface.

NFs are influencers, empathetic, passionate, emotional, sensitive, introspective, and lovers of harmony among people. Mostly they are perfectionists, self-demanding, idealists, imaginative, and visionaries living in the world of dreams (both practical and fanciful). To these self-actualizers, life must have meaning and significance.
Does this describe you best?

If you are still puzzled or unsure of which temperament you are and which describes you best, then go to my book, *INNERKINETICS - Your blueprint to Excellence and Happiness*, and all should soon become clear.

A Few Suggested Books For Further Reading

Michael J. Behe, *Darwin's Black Box*
　　　　Darwin Devolves
David Horowitz, *Dark Agenda*
Ray W. Lincoln, *Compelling Evidence for God*
　　　　I'm a Keeper
　　　　InnerKinetics
Gad Saad, *The Parasitic Mind*
Francis A. Schaeffer, *How Should We Then Live*

About The Author

Ray W. Lincoln is the bestselling author of *I'm a Keeper* and *INNERKINETICS* and is the founder of Ray W. Lincoln & Associates. Ray is a professional life coach and an expert in human nature. His 40 plus years of experience in speaking, teaching, and counseling began in New Zealand and have carried him to Australia and the United States. He speaks with energy and enthusiasm before large and small audiences.

It was not by accident that he became the international speaker and coach that he is today and acquired the ability to help individuals and help parents understand their children. Ray has studied extensively in the fields of Philosophy, Temperament Psychology, and Personology. A member of the National Speakers Association, his expertise has been used as a lecturer and professor, teacher, keynote speaker, and seminar presenter. He teaches and leads in staff trainings, university student retreats, and parenting and educational classes as well as other seminars and training events. He also trains and mentors teachers and other professionals and executives — all with the goal of understanding our own temperaments and those of others.

Ray lives with his wife, Mary Jo, in Ingram, Texas, where they enjoy hiking, gardening, birdwatching, and all the beauty the Texas Hill Country offers. Both are highly involved in their work, which they feel is the most important and most fulfilling work of their entire career lives, each filling the role for which they were designed as they travel to speak to groups and to present seminars and workshops throughout the US.

www.ingramcontent.com/pod-product-compliance
Lightning Source LLC
Chambersburg PA
CBHW060253100426
42742CB00011B/1732